The Land and People of
POLAND

The colorful and sometimes tragic past of Poland unfolds in strik-
ing chapters filled with fascinating bits of folklore and custom.
There are rich descriptions of the historic old cities of Krakow and
Warsaw as they were and as they are today.

In this newly revised edition we are brought up to date on a
country where liberties which others take for granted are those
for which the Poles are struggling.

PORTRAITS OF THE NATIONS SERIES

Also in the same format

The Land and People of
POLAND

by Eric P. Kelly
revised by Dragos D. Kostich

REVISED EDITION 1972

PORTRAITS OF THE NATIONS SERIES

J. B. LIPPINCOTT COMPANY
Philadelphia   New York

The pictures on pages 50, bottom, 108, 111, 113, and 124 are from Wide World Photos; on page 64 from Eastfoto; on pages 29, 39, 56, 59, 65, 69, 72, 73, 77, 81, 84, bottom, 86, 92, top, 96, and 99, courtesy of the Polish Embassy; on pages 17, 68, 119, and 125 courtesy of ORBIS, the Polish Travel Office.

U. S. Library of Congress Cataloging in Publication Data

Kelly, Eric Philbrook, birth date
  The land and people of Poland.

  (Portraits of the nations series)
  Summary: An introduction to the geography, people, culture, and turbulent history of Poland, a communist satellite nation.
  First published in 1943 under title: The land of the Polish people.

  1. Poland—Juvenile literature. [1. Poland] I. Kostich, Dragoš D. II. Title.
DK404.K4   1972   914.38   73-37924
ISBN-0-397-31313-6   ISBN-0-397-31206-7 (lib. bdg.)

Map by Gruger Studio

Contents

The Land and People of
POLAND

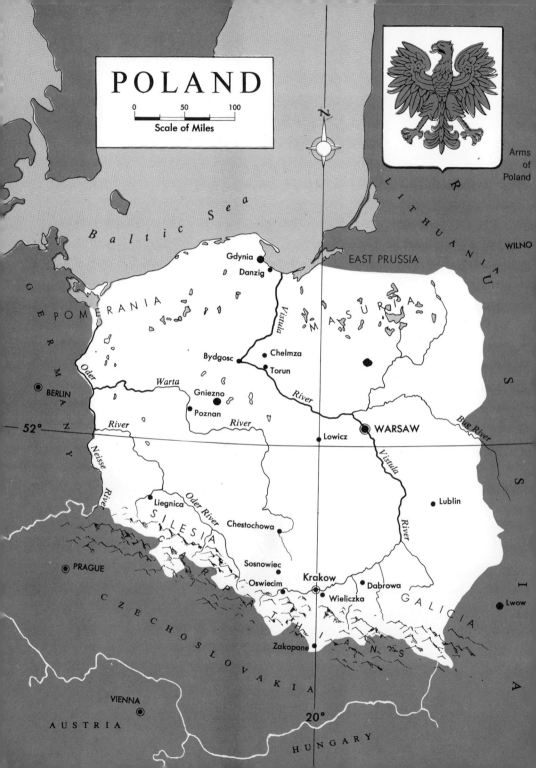

POLAND

0   50   100
Scale of Miles

Arms
of
Poland

Baltic Sea

GERMANY

POMERANIA

Oder River

BERLIN

52°

Neisse River

Warta River

Gniezno

Poznan

Liegnica

SILESIA

Oder River

PRAGUE

CZECHOSLOVAKIA

VIENNA

AUSTRIA

Gdynia

Danzig

EAST PRUSSIA

LITHUANIA

WILNO

Vistula

MASURIA

Bydgosc

Chelmza

Torun

River

R   U   S   S   I   A

Lowicz

WARSAW

Bug River

Vistula River

Lublin

Chestochowa

Sosnowiec

Oswiecim

Krakow

Wieliczka

Dabrowa

GALICIA

Lwow

CARPATHIANS

Zakopane

HUNGARY

20°

1

The Land of Legend

POLAND IS a Slavonic country. In fact, Poland's modern borders include regions that were the ancestral home of the Slavs in remote antiquity. From these regions, centered in the Pripet Marsh in southeastern Poland, early Slavs migrated eastward to create Russia, westward to Czechoslovakia and adjoining areas, and southward to the Balkan Peninsula where they eventually created the countries of Bulgaria and Yugoslavia. The ancestors of the people of Poland were mainly the Slavs who did not migrate.

Who were the early Slavs, in what kind of a country did they live, what was their life like, and why did some of them migrate to faraway lands while others did not? To-day, lengthy studies in history, supported by archaeological research and studies of the nature and origins of modern European languages, provide us with answers to many questions about earlier times. Curiously enough, the way in which people lived, spoke, and faced problems then, has a bearing on their life now in most cases.

Like most Europeans, the Slavs are of Indo-European stock. And like the Celts or the Greeks and Romans, they came to Europe from southern Asia long before man's recorded history began. All land was then sparsely populated. In Europe, however, there were other, now unknown, people—people who left signs of themselves in the Stone Age arrowheads and tools scattered in hunting grounds throughout Europe, or remnants of their simple pottery found near the long-extinguished hearths where they once lived; or people who left splendid cave paintings in France and Spain.

In southeastern Poland there was a culture called the "Lusatian Culture." It ended suddenly about 500 B.C., and was replaced by a different culture. It is not known if the people of the Lusatian Culture were Slavs, who were superseded by other Slavs, or if a Slavonic invasion caused the disappearance of an earlier group. But the evidence available allows us to conclude two things: first, the Slavs did inhabit permanently the regions of southeastern Poland after 500 B.C., and second, the Slavs had been present in the adjoining regions before 500 B.C. They expanded northward and westward a short time later. Slowly but steadily they settled in the area which is now in Poland, and beyond it, almost as far as Berlin in Germany.

For a long time, the Slavs settled neither to the east nor to the south of southeastern Poland. We don't know why they did not move into the almost empty Russian plain to the east of them. They must have known about it, for it is through that plain that they migrated to the Pripet Marsh area. Were they trying to stay as far away as possible from the fierce Scythian horsemen who lived in the open southern Russian prairie, the *steppe?* Perhaps. But we do know why the Slavs did not move southward. Just south and southwest of the Pripet Marsh area rise the high mountains, the Tatra Mountains, which form the northern arm of the Carpathian Range. This is a horseshoe-shaped ranged, with its northern arm extending eastward from the modern Czechoslovak-German border in the west; then in southeasternmost Poland the mountains run due south, and then again west to reach the lower Danube. Cradled within this horseshoe-shaped range, which opens to the west, is the Hungarian Plain. Beyond the Tatra Mountains, to the south in what is now Czechoslovakia, there were the early Germanic tribes: the Boii, after whom modern Bohemia has been named, and later on the migrating Goths, dangerous warriors.

As Greece rose and declined, and as Rome built its empire, the Slavs in the remote regions north of the Carpathians lived unperturbed and largely untouched by the brilliant, turbulent, great civilizations of the Mediterranean. Greek and Roman geographers and historians were aware of the Slavs. Ptolemy and others wrote about the faraway people and their customs, as they heard of them from occasional traders who ventured into a world little known to them. So little was known about the early Slavs that the Greek and Roman scholars referred to them by the name of one or another tribe that travelers had encountered; they called them the *Venedi,* or the *Bulanes* (a mispronounciation of the *Poliane,* a large tribe who eventually gave its name to Poland), or *Sorabes* (a mispronounciation of "Serbs"), and so on. As for the Slavs, they called themselves *Sloviane*.

In most modern Slavonic languages, the word *slovo* means a written or printed character, or a word. In Old Slavonic, however, this term had a broader meaning, and in medieval Polish, Russian, or Serbian, slovo could mean a story, or a poem, or even speech. The early Slavs called themselves *Sloviane,* using the term to describe all those who spoke the same language, nothing more than that. They didn't think of themselves as Slavs, but as members of this or that tribe, or even more as belonging to a particular clan.

Their whole society was based upon the clan and the tribe, and they governed themselves by a system often called "patriarchal democracy." Each clan consisted of a number of *extended* families. This means that a family included not only the parents and their children, but uncles and aunts, many cousins, grandparents, and often great-grandparents. The adult members chose among themselves the head of the family. This, as a rule, was the person who was respected and obeyed above any other in the family—it could be a woman, although it was usually a man. The respect was probably based on the family's admiration of this person's wisdom. Once chosen a family head, this person had almost absolute authority over all other members. It was he, or she, who assigned the various jobs to each member, sat in judgment of disputes, and decided who would get how much of the extended family's harvest. For in this society the individual owned only his personal possessions, clothes and such, but everything else belonged to the family as a whole—fields and tools, animals and the produce of their farms. A person alone could not survive long under the circumstances in which they lived. Survival was feasible only within the family, and even within the clan and the tribe.

Families belonging to one clan lived near to each other. As a rule, one clan would form a village, but if it was a large clan, there would be several villages, all close by. The clan was governed by a council of the heads of families. Their chosen representatives spoke for them in the tribal council, and elected the tribe's chieftain. The chieftain could be removed from office at any time by the tribal council, and his power was very limited. He could not declare war, for example, nor make any important decision without the tribal council's approval.

Tacitus, the Roman historian of antiquity, wrote about the Slavs, whom he called the *Venedi,* claiming that although they lived very much like many other nomadic tribal societies, they were "not nomads, because they build permanent houses." It is true that they built permanent dwellings, yet they were at least partly nomadic. This had to do with the early Slavs' method of farming, which was rather wasteful.

Southeastern Poland, their ancestral land, is a land of rivers and lakes and, even now, deep forests. The early Slavs would make clearings in the forest to use as fields for their crops. Rather than go to the trouble of felling huge trees with their primitive tools, they made the clearings by setting fire to underbrush and trees. This cleared the forest quickly, but it left all the roots in the soil, making it impossible to plow deep furrows. This didn't bother the Slavs. Instead of plowing, they farmed mostly by scratching the surface with their hoes, and then planting the seed. But the soil which had not been plowed, and of which only the uppermost layer was used, lost its nutrients after four or five harvests. It could be farmed successfully again only if it was allowed to lie fallow for ten or fifteen years, so that nature could restore the minerals and other ingredients which had been exhausted through farming.

This did not worry the early Slavs either. When their clearings became exhausted, the clan simply moved on in search of some other part of the forest that had not been taken over by anyone else, and there they would repeat the process of making new clearings, farming, and moving on after four or five years. Sometimes they returned to their earlier clearings, after the land had recuperated by lying fallow for many years.

Wherever they went, the Slavs either built or returned

to the dwellings they had occupied earlier. These were the "houses" that Tacitus spoke of. In fact, they were what are now called "pit dwellings," and they are remarkably adapted to the climate and way of life of the early Slavs. Archeological excavations have uncovered traces of many such dwellings.

An extended family would first dig several adjoining pits in the soft, moist earth, square in shape and three or four feet deep. Then, along the sides of each pit, they would erect low walls made of logs, and then cover the pit with a thatched roof. Now each pit became a room, and was connected by short passageways not only to the family's other rooms, but also to roofed pits prepared for their farm animals—their barns and stables. Each room in which people lived had a fireplace and a chimneylike device, dug in the side of one wall of the pit, where they cooked their meals or warmed themselves during the long, cold, windy winters.

These dwellings of extended families belonging to one clan were connected by covered trenches, so people could go back and forth even in the worst weather without having to go outdoors. A clan's village covered perhaps two or three acres—all pit dwellings and stables, and all interconnected, rather like a huge rabbit warren, where people and animals inside were warm and safe.

If the clan returned to an earlier site even ten or fifteen years later, all they had to do was repair the roofs and they had their homes ready. So Tacitus was right when he wrote that the Slavs built permanent "houses," but he was only partly right when he claimed that they were not nomadic. Rather, their society was an unusual one, and different from most other tribal societies of that time.

In their religion, however, the early Slavs were very similar to most central and northern European tribal people of that time. They believed in many gods, and their deities represented either the forces of nature or the hopes and fears of man. Their supreme deity was Perun, god of thunder and lightning. Vesna was their goddess of Spring, who regenerated nature, youth, beauty, and learning—she embodied their hopes. Morana, the goddess of Winter, darkness, and death, embodied their fears. Among other major deities there was Veles, their cattle-god; because of him we know today that the early Slavs not only kept, but largely depended on, cattle, which makes them rather different from many of their contemporaries who still depended mainly on hunting for their food supply.

Moving at intervals from site to site, the early Slavs did not build permanent temples for worshiping their gods. Instead, they worshiped in sacred oak groves, or at home. Each family had its own patron deity who protected it from the wrath of Perun and other major deities. The family maintained a small altar, usually by the fireplace, where it prayed to its patron deity and made sacrificial offerings of wheat and honey to its protector.

Honey was important in the life of the early Slavs, who were renowned as beekeepers—and it is still important in Poland's countryside, where few farms do not have beehives in their back yard or nearby. The Slavs used honey for sweetening their food—sugar was unknown to them

—and for brewing strong mead which they drank on festive occasions.

In addition to major and minor deities, the early Slavs believed in the existence of all kinds of creatures with supernatural powers. They believed that they were surrounded by invisible jinns, tiny creatures not unlike leprechauns, who were the source of all mischief and minor accidents that could not be explained otherwise. Much more important were the water nymphs. On certain moonlit nights young women of extraordinary beauty could be seen by men usually dancing in some lovely field by a lake or a stream—a sight worthy of a young man's dream. However, those who dared look at them were severely punished for their indiscretion, and either disappeared forever or were made insane by the angered

Neptune fountain in Gdansk.

nymphs. On the other hand, the nymphs, who were believed to know everyone's thoughts as well as actions, could reward discretion or bravery by awarding wisdom to a man or by making him safe in the face of his enemies.

Unlike almost all of their European contemporaries, the early Slavs had few enemies. The Carpathian Range sheltered them in the south from invasions and devastations that accompanied the Great Migration after the second century A.D. The immense space of the Russian plain and the dense woodlands north of the open Russian steppe protected them from the dangerous nomad warriors who rode from Central Asia westward—the Huns, the Avars, and the people who later called themselves the Magyars, who raided and devastated Europe all the way to the gates of Paris, Rome, and Constantinople. Of these only the last wave, Genghis Khan's Mongols, struck at Poland beginning in the late 1230's, but by then Poland was strong enough to assure its survival despite the immense danger it faced.

To the northeast of the Slavs were the sparsely populated lands on the shores of the Baltic Sea, inhabited by ancestors of modern Lithuanians. All major rivers of Poland flow north to the Baltic. At times the Baltic shore was visited, and occasionally raided, by the ancestors of the Vikings, who were great seamen and fierce warriors. Sometimes they sailed up the rivers deep into Poland, and the Slavs either traded or fought with them, depending on circumstances. Far to the west, beyond the deep forests of Saxony, which were virtually impenetrable even in Charlemagne's time at the end of the eighth century A.D., there were the Germanic tribes. Numerous and powerful, but constantly at war with Rome, the Germans were then in the process of migration south and west. Not until centuries later did the Slavs of Poland clash with the Germans, who then were among their main adversaries.

So the early Slavonic world was a peaceful one, like a remote, quiet island in a sea of turbulence. Even centuries later, a Byzantine traveler recorded in wonderment that travelers in the Slavonic lands carried no weapons but only a musical instrument, a lute or a harp, so safe was the land. One of the reasons that it was so safe, the chronicler added, was the unavoidable and savage blood vendetta. If someone killed a person, even accidentally, unless peace was made the family that lost a member was honor bound to avenge him by killing either the murderer or any male member of his family. More often than not, the offender's family forced him to surrender and be judged, rather than face a vendetta which could be erased neither by time nor by flight. So certain was this vendetta that few dared to commit acts of violence among the Slavs.

Their methods of warfare, and even their weapons, reflected this peaceful nature of their world. They had no weapons or techniques for offensive warfare and conquest, but only for defense. They had practically no cavalry, nor could cavalry be used in the forests they inhabited. Their weapons were short swords and javelins, bows and arrows with arrowheads often dipped in a poisonous brew made of the root of wolfsbane and other now unknown ingredients, and slingshots, which they used with extraordinary accuracy. As for the poisoned arrow-heads, there is a record of a Byzantine emperor who died of a wound from one. The poison apparently produced the immediate effect of a rather pleasant sense of tired-ness, followed by sleep from which the victim never awoke.

When defending their homes, the early Slavs would usually ambush the enemy somewhere in the forest, striking from treetops and, on foot, from the under-growth. Sometimes they even laid an ambush underwater. They were known for their ability to stay concealed in shallow water while breathing through hollow reeds, and they would suddenly strike at the enemy as if coming from nowhere.

Why did so many Slavonic tribes leave this quiet land to settle elsewhere? The most likely answer is that they simply had to. By the fifth century A.D., the Slavonic regions in Poland had become overpopulated. The land could no longer feed the people—not with the wasteful farming practices of the early Slavs. The clans and tribes moved on in search of unoccupied land, and each wavelet of migration went a little farther out than the preceding one. They moved out farther and farther, until it became impracticable for more and more of them to return to their earlier sites. Some followed the rivers of Russia until they populated that great plain. Others moved west-ward or southwestward, crossed the northern branch of the Carpathian Range, and settled in regions now in Czechoslovakia or Germany and Austria. Yet others, moving southward, were caught up in the turmoil of the

Hungarian plain, where the Goths and the Huns and many other migrating peoples from Europe and Asia sought to establish a foothold, and the Slavs eventually broke away into the Byzantine imperial provinces in the Balkans, and settled there.

Some Slavonic tribes, however, did not leave their ancestral land, and their descendants founded Poland. Finally the *Poliane* tribe united them in the 960's to found modern Poland—Poliane simply means "Lowlanders," or the tribe that lives in fields rather than woodlands. Other early groups in Poland referred to themselves as the *Lechs*. This name may be derived from the Old Slavonic word *les,* meaning "forest"—the tribe that lives in the woodlands. In Poland there remains a keen awareness of this distant past, which is told in the form of stories and legends.

This is how the old grandmother—the *babushka*, as the children affectionately called her—sitting before the fire during the long winter told her children and grandchildren about the Slav people. There were, she said, three brothers who lived together in the rich northern land of the Vistula Valley. Their names were Lech, Czech, and Rus. Now after a while their lands became so prosperous, and their flocks so great, that there was not enough room for them to live side by side. Therefore they had to separate and each seek a new land where there was space for the great families and flocks.

So, in order to look about and pick out good places for them all, Lech decided to climb a tree and see what he could see. From the very high branches he looked out to the east and saw rich river valleys, fertile steppes or prairies, a vast stretch of land. Whereupon he shouted this information down to his brothers.

"That's the land for me," said Brother Rus. "East I will go." And so he went, and today his people, the Russians, live on the great plains by the rivers.

Again Lech looked away, this time to the south. "I see a land of mountains and plains," he shouted. "On the north is a great wall that will protect anyone from his enemies. There is plenty of water and beyond the mountains many plains. The sun is much warmer there than here."

"That's the land for me," said Brother Czech. And so he departed for the land to the south, which today we know as Czechoslovakia.

Lech was now left alone. He didn't know quite what to do. He looked to the north, but saw only the sea. He looked to the west and saw only forests and strange tribes dwelling among them. "I don't want to go there," he thought, "but where *can* I go?"

As he was puzzling over his problem, something attached to the tree caught his eye. "A bird's nest," he exclaimed. Then he thought really hard, for an idea had come to him. "Perhaps I was meant to see that," he reasoned. "Perhaps that will help me decide." So he took the empty nest in his hand, for the birds had already left it, and descended.

Just as his feet touched the earth, he suddenly understood what it all meant. . . . "Why," he said to himself, "the nest means that this very place is my home. Here I will live. Here will be my nest." So he called the place Gniezno, meaning "nest," and not only was it the first town in Poland, but it retains its name to this day and is honored by Poles all over the world. In the nearby city of Poznan the first capital of Poland was set up, and it has been the seat of the Primate of the Church, bishop or archbishop, since that day.

Grandmother has another story about the southwestern corner of Poland, for Poland has what its people call four corners, Poznan, Krakow, Lwow, and Wilno, the last being the old capital of Lithuania, and shared by Lithuanian and Pole for hundreds of years.

In the southwestern corner of Poland is the city of Krakow. In early days, these rich lands near the Vistula as it comes from the Carpathians were not lived in very much, because a frightful dragon lived there, grandmother says—a great long animal with a huge body and jaws like those of an immense lizard, breathing fire, scorching the lands, and burning up the people.

Many great warriors tried to kill this dragon, but all were instead killed by him. However, there lived in this land a youth by the name of Krakus, who had an idea that he could remove this dragon from the valley. So he went up to the top of a hill, called the Wawel, one day, when the dragon was safely away, and found the animal's cave. This cave one may explore today. It runs from the top of the Wawel clear down underground to the very bank of the river.

Krakus looked the ground over and made his decision. He knew that it was not worth while to fight the dragon with a sword, for the flames coming out of the monster's mouth would burn up anyone within fifty feet of him. So he went over to an old mine where the Lechs dug sulphur, and loaded many skins full of it and carried them back to the cave, one by one. Then he took the huge carcass of an ox and filled it full of the sulphur he had brought. He left it at the river's edge on the path which the dragon was accustomed to taking.

Next he had to hide and watch, and this is what took place.

The dragon came back from a hunt, evidently hungry, for he hadn't captured anything to eat, and the first thing he saw was the carcass by the river. Without stopping to examine it closely, he gulped it down, sulphur and all.

Still breathing fire, he lay down to sleep, but, all at once, began to feel uncomfortable inside. His stomach seemed to grow hotter and hotter, and finally more flames than usual burst from his mouth. Disturbed and alarmed, he rushed down to the river to drink, but the minute he took a mouthful, the sulphur in the meat which he had eaten burst into flames, and before Krakus could realize that he was successful, the dragon was nothing but a heap of black coals.

Then the families in the valley all rushed down to the fertile lands and settled there. The dragon would bother them no longer. And they made Krakus the king, and gave his name to the new city which they were founding on the hill, and when he died they built a huge mound of earth as a monument to him. It lies just outside the city walls, and may be seen today.

Grandmother has another story about the city of Wilno in the northeast corner. In the early days the Poles and Lithuanians living there were much bothered by another monster who also breathed fire, a monster that they called the Basilichek. This creature was in the habit of destroying all their flocks and burning their fields, and no one could destroy him. It seems that he was so ugly that anyone who desired to fight him died immediately at the mere sight of him.

A boy on one of the farms figured out something that he thought might work. Everyone told him he was foolish to try to kill the Basilichek, because one couldn't look at him to fight him, and what's the use of fighting if you don't get a chance to see your enemy?

He insisted, however, and so they gave him some armor, a sword and a shield, and a helmet. He took all these and thanked his friends, but when he was out in the country near the cave of the Basilichek, he threw away the sword and helmet and kept only the shield. This was very large, extending from his neck to his feet almost, but he went straight to work, polishing the inside of it so briskly that it shone like a mirror, and indeed became a mirror.

Then he concealed himself directly in front of the cave where the monster lived. He knew that the Basilichek was inside for he could see flames issuing from the cave's mouth. All one night he waited, eagerly watching for the dawn when the fierce animal would come out to kill the sheep and burn the crops with his fiery breath.

The sun rose. There was a stir in the cave, then a great roar as the monster crawled to his feet and started for the cave's mouth. At the sound, the youth began to tremble. He wondered if there was still time to run away. But then he thought of his plan, of the armor his friends had found for him, and he decided to stay. So he turned the mirror side of the shield toward the cave's mouth, and squatted down behind it. The next instant, the Basilichek was outside in the daylight.

The boy closed his eyes, but he clung to the shield. What would happen now? If his plan did not work, he certainly would be dead in a very short time. So he waited and waited, for what seemed like centuries, although it was but a few minutes.

At first, the Basilichek, seeing the shield, let out a roar. Then he dashed upon it to demolish it. But all of a sudden he stopped dead in his tracks! And then, with hardly a groan, he rolled over on his side and died, just as the boy had planned. The sight of his own ugly visage reflected in the shining shield had been the end of him, just as it had killed so many people in the past.

Around this hill over the dragon's cave, so the legend goes, grew up the great city of Wilno, a lovely city, dear to Lithuanians and Poles alike.

Grandmother has more stories, and all have to do with the ancient Lechs who became the Poles. Since there is no written record of the early years, one must study and think about these tales as they are, and realize that they probably held a truth and meaning for people living many years ago which we, today, do not fully understand.

2

The Land of Destiny

AND NOW SLOWLY there arose upon the borders of what
men thought of as the civilized world the new country of
Poland.

It was small at first, back in those days of 965 A.D.
when the first Polish king, Mieszko, was baptized, and
married the daughter of the king of Bohemia. He was one
of the kings of the Piast line, the first Polish rulers, with
his capital at the city of Poznan in the northwest corner
of the country.

The early Piast kings were of peasant stock, farmers.
There are many stories of this family, preserved as legend,
one of them being of the original Piast who sheltered a
weary traveler from the rain, and found on the morning

that his guest had departed, leaving him a golden crown.

After the crowning of the first king, Poland grew by leaps and bounds, and it became necessary to move the capital south to Krakow, which had become a large and prosperous city. But Poles have a great affection for Poznan, and resent very much the name "Corridor" which was applied by the Prussians to the northern provinces, particularly as these provinces form the oldest part of the country.

In the thirteenth century Poland was devastated by the Tartars, who swept in from Asia in the days of Genghis Khan. But in the fourteenth century there rose to power a brave and warlike people, the Lithuanians, who with the Poles fought off the Tartars and drove them clear back out of the western Slav lands. It followed that a unity of Poles and Lithuanians was desired by many people, and the result was the marriage of the Polish queen, Jadwiga, one of Poland's most beloved rulers, and the Grand Duke, Ladislaus Jagiello, of Lithuania. Thus the two countries were united, and the new confederation extended clear from the Black Sea to the Baltic, from eastern Germany to the Dnieper River in the land of the old Rus.

Jadwiga, a young girl at the time of the proposed marriage, had already set her heart upon another husband. At one time, rebelling at the situation, and desiring to escape from the castle in Krakow to seek the man of her choice, she took a battle-axe from the castle wall, and began to hew at one of the heavy doors. An old counsellor happened to hear the noise and, coming down the steps,

A modern painting of the arrival of the Bohemian princess Do-brawa, the future wife of the first Polish king, Mieszko I.

discovered what the young queen was trying to do. He was able to reason with her, and make her understand what a deed of patriotism her marriage with Jagiello would be, since the union of the two countries stood for a powerful force against invasion. Because of her great love for Poland, she finally yielded. Though she did not live long after the marriage, her charity and generosity were so great that she is known to the present time as Poland's sainted queen.

One important act, never to be forgotten in her country, was the gift of her jewels to the new University of Krakow, which was struggling along, proverty-stricken and powerless.

Many stories are told of Jadwiga—one having to do with her great fondness for dogs. When a man had said of another man that he "lied like a dog," she promptly issued orders that the offender stand in the market-place and bark like a dog for one whole day, letting it be known emphatically that dogs do not lie. When she died, a sculptor carved a statue of her in marble, and this lies over her tomb. Tucked up in the robes of marble at her feet is a little white dog.

Krakow had become a beautiful city by Jadwiga's time. Her grandfather, Kazimir the Great, had torn down most of the wooden buildings, and replaced them with stone.

A long line of Lithuanian kings followed Ladislaus and Jadwiga on the Polish throne. Under them, cities were built, the countryside was improved, the Vistula was filled with little rafts bearing merchandise to and from the great port of Danzig which the Polish king opened to the Hanse merchants as a free port. But though the country was flourishing, nations on the borders were continually pressing in and trying to take Polish lands, and war followed war in quick succession. In spite of all this warfare, at the height of its greatness in the fifteenth and sixteenth centuries, the Polish-Lithuanian federation, called the Commonwealth, was the greatest power in central Europe, and one of the great powers of the world.

And as Poland stood on the border, it defended western Europe from armies that poured through from Asia. At first it was the Tartars, then next the Turks, and when the Polish armies under Sobieski at Vienna defeated the Turks in 1685 it ended all European invasions from the east. This was the beginning of the two-hundred-year-long withdrawal of the Turkish empire from the conquered European countries.

But Poland had suffered in these wars. Many of her lands and towns had been destroyed, many of her people had been killed. And when hostilities broke out in Europe in which were involved Austrians, Prussians, Russians, Swedes, Bohemians, and even French and English, Poland was often the battleground. Each locality had to have its own great castle for defense; each town and district had to have its own army.

The Polish people are essentially democratic and freedom loving, and like the Greeks and the Swiss had worked out a system of choosing their leaders by vote of all land-holding citizens. The citizens used to assemble in a great field outside of Warsaw, and each district would come in and cast its vote. Once the vote was for a French prince, but he soon tired of ruling people whom he did not understand and made a disgraceful flight by night from the capital city. After Sobieski, three kings were elected in succession from the neighboring German province of Saxony.

In the reign of Sigismund the Third (1587-1632) of the Swedish House of Vasa, the capital was removed to Warsaw. This was necessary because of the more central location of the new city, adjacent to the province of Prussia and to the Principality of Wilno. In Warsaw, near the Cathedral and the King's palace, there stood in a square the statue of Sigismund on a high pillar. The king bore a sword in his hand, and it was an old belief in Poland that when a war approached, the king's sword would be lowered. Some people even say that they saw it lowered in 1914. The statue was destroyed in 1944.

Affairs in Poland had not been going well in the earlier years of the eighteenth century. Enemies on the border were gaining more and more strength. The power of the king had been greatly lessened by the private armies that each of the great nobles had, and it was hard to get them all together for common defense. Thus, by the time the last king of Poland, Stanislaus Poniatowski, came to the throne in 1764, the fate of Poland was sealed. Russia marched in and occupied part of her territory. Austria took another part, and Prussia a third.

At this moment, however, in Polish history, appeared a man who is important in the history of both Poland and the United States. He was Thaddeus Kosciuszko, a brilliant young nobleman from Poland who became dedicated to the ideals of liberty and constitutional government of the American Revolution. Educated in military academies in Warsaw and Paris, Kosciuszko studied military engineering and construction of fortifications. When the American War of Independence began, Kosciuszko left Europe at once and offered his services to George Washington. Other Polish patriots followed Kosciuszko to America. Especially remembered are those led by Casimir Pulaski, who became a brigadier general in the American Revolutionary Army. General Pulaski died in 1779 while leading a cavalry charge at Savannah, Georgia. Kosciuszko survived many battles, fought mainly in New York and in the Carolinas. It was he who fortified West Point and constructed a chain across the Hudson to keep the British fleet from sailing upstream from New York and cutting the American forces in two. It was Kosciuszko again who was instrumental in persuading Thomas Jefferson to set up a military academy at West Point.

But Kosciuszko and many other Polish volunteers who had fought in the American War of Independence did not intend to stay in the United States. They had left their beleaguered homeland in order to help the Americans because they believed deeply in their ideals. Once this war was won, they returned to Poland in order to fight for the same ideals there. After five years in America, Kosciuszko returned home in 1792. He found Poland on the threshold of disaster.

Russia, Prussia, and Austria had each taken a part of

Poland, in 1772. This is called the First Partitioning. But Poland, although weakened, tried desperately to secure its survival by making many reforms and by developing an excellent educational system—a system that helped train more people like Kosciuszko and Pulaski. Poland's recovery was not to her neighbors' taste and, in 1792, they were about to partition it again. This was not merely a matter of rapacity. The empires of Russia and Austria and the kingdom of Prussia feared the spreading in Poland of precisely those ideas and ideals which had made Kosciuszko and Pulaski go to fight for the American cause. They tried to divide Poland internally, and to have the supporters of royal absolutism fight the constitutionalists. Kosciuszko placed himself at the head of an army of insurgents, mostly poorly armed peasants, and took up the fight against his adversaries, who were aided by the Russian and Prussian armies. He was defeated in this uneven struggle. The end came when, in the last great battle, he was shot from his horse and taken prisoner by the Russians in 1793. The whole spirit of the insurgency died, the Second Partitioning of Poland took place, and in 1795 the Third Partitioning wiped out what was left of Poland. Poland was erased from the political map of Europe, but the ideals of liberty exemplified in Kosciuszko's struggle lived on and helped bring about Poland's rebirth in 1918.

As for Kosciuszko, he was released from Russian captivity in 1796, but was not allowed to return to Poland. He went back to America but soon came to feel he was too far removed from Poland and its travail, so he returned to Europe. Throughout the great upheavals of the Napoleonic Wars Kosciuszko stayed in France, trying to win freedom for his country, but there was no hope. He died in 1817, an exile in Switzerland. Only then did the Russians allow Kosciuszko's body to be brought back to Poland, where he was buried in Cracow.

For 123 years the Poles remained a nation without a country. Poland was divided into three parts among Austria, Russia, and Prussia, all of which became a part of the German Empire in 1872. In some parts even the use of the Polish language in public schools was forbidden —but neither the language, nor the ideals of liberty, nor the hope for independence, was forgotten. In 1917, in the midst of World War I, one of the points of President Wilson's Fourteen Points message was of great importance to Poland. This Point stated that the Allies were fighting the war in order to secure the right of self-determination for all nations. Poland, President Wilson declared, must be free again, and it must have access to the sea. In 1918, as World War I ended, Poland declared its independence.

From 1918 to 1939, Poland underwent intensive development. The school system was extended to reach every town and village; Polish universities saw their international reputation for learning being restored. Many new industries were added to the existing ones—which now included shipbuilding and automobile and aircraft manufacturing—and new roads, railroads, and bridges sprang up throughout the land. A new port rose on the site of a tiny fishing village at Gdynia on the Baltic Sea,

Poland's only access to the oceans, and Polish ships sailed from there to ply the seas of the world.

There were problems, of course. The gravest of them involved Poland's borders with her two mighty neighbors —Russia in the east, and Germany in the west. After the Third Partitioning of Poland, the character of the population in some previously Polish border provinces was changed, sometimes forcibly. A century later, the Poles had become a minority in some of the regions where they had been the majority. Newly independent Poland felt that these provinces should be Polish again, because the changes in population had been made unfairly during the time when Poland was partitioned and helpless.

At the Paris Peace Conference in 1919, Germany was forced to yield to Poland the Polish Corridor, a narrow strip of land which connected Poland with her port at Gdynia but which separated the German province of East Prussia from Germany proper. At the same time, an international commission headed by Lord Curzon awarded to Russia large parts of the once Polish eastern provinces, which were by now inhabited mostly by Byelorussians and Ukrainians. In 1920, Poland and the USSR fought a brief but bitter war over these borders. Although peace was signed in 1921, this remained an issue which would haunt Poland later on.

The issue of the Polish Corridor became serious soon after 1933, when Hitler took power in Germany. It was under the pretext of this issue that Nazi Germany attacked Poland in 1939.

3

A Nation of Song

"Poland still is not forgotten
While her sons remain.
Honor out of shame begotten
Let our swords proclaim."

Free translation of the opening lines
of the Polish National Anthem.

So SANG THE SOLDIERS of the Polish Legions as they marched in Europe in the armies of Napoleon. So sang the soldiers of the Haller Legion as they marched with the French and English and Americans in the First World War of 1914-1918. So sang the Poles as they marched and flew and rode in all the armies of the Allies during World War II.

Yet they sang and sang and still sing, and from among them have arisen some of the most able musicians of all time. It is quite notable that one of their greatest men, Ignace Paderewski, was as eminent a statesman as he was a pianist and composer. In every farm, in every village, in the old court of the kings, and on the dance-hall floor of the market-town, Poles danced and sang from the beginning of time. There was the Polonaise, a dance which came from the royal court; the Mazur, with its little figures, or Mazurkas, which has become the country's national dance. There was the Krakowiak with its familiar cadence which every musician knows. But the working people and the farmers loved the Polka, a word meaning a Polish dance, since the name of their country in their own language is Polska.

They sang as they worked. There was a song of the mill as its wheel turned around; there was the song of the scythe as it swept through the wheat; there was the song of the little cudgel as the women beat the clothes dry with it after laundering them in a pool at the backdoor of every village. The shepherd in the Carpathians played his pipe as the sheep followed their leader over the stony slopes. The wayfarer often marched along the road, violin in hand, his long dusty coat hanging about his bare feet, playing some forgotten tune as his eyes were lost in the skies. The girl sang as she drove the sheep home at night, the drovers chanted as they drove the cattle to market.

One of the greatest Polish musicians, Frederick Chopin, took all these melodies and worked them into magnificent compositions that let the world know something of what

Learning to dance, a favorite pastime of the Poles.

was in the Polish heart. Even before he was twenty years old, he had become famous for his piano concerts in Warsaw, Vienna, and Munich, as well as for his early compositions.

In 1830, despairing of their future in the partitioned land, the Polish people in the regions held by Russia rose against their oppressors. Once again, this was a bitter, uneven struggle between dedicated patriots and powerful imperial armies. At first the Poles were successful and even liberated Warsaw. In 1831, however, they were defeated by the Russians, and even what little self-government there had been heretofore in Poland was terminated. With thousands of patriots, young Chopin emigrated from Poland. He was not to see his homeland again. He spent the rest of his life fighting on in his own way. People in the Western World could not understand Polish, perhaps, but they could listen to music, and so Chopin told the world the story of Poland in music. There one finds all the splendor of the court of the kings, there one finds the sadness of a conquered people marching to the grave, for the Chopin funeral march is just that, and not the funeral march of just one person. In the music of Chopin one hears the guns of Napoleon roaring, as the Polish legions approach Poland and home again, with his armies, in the spring of 1812.

What a year that was for Polish hopes. What expectations were everywhere aroused that Napoleon had come to free them from Prussia and Austria and Russia. As it says in the finest of the Polish national poems, *Pan Tadeusz,* by Adam Mickiewicz:

"The year 1812! Memorable year. Happy is he who

Carpathian shepherds calling their sheep with trumpets.

beheld thee in our land. The folk still call thee the year of harvest, but the soldiers the year of war. Old men still love to tell tales of thee, and poets still dream of thee. . . . Steeds, men, cannon, eagles, flowed on day and night; here and there fires glowed in the sky; the earth trembled, in the distance one could hear the rolling of thunder.

"War! War! There was no corner in the land to which its roar did not reach; amidst dark forests the peasant, whose grandfathers and kinsmen had died without seeing beyond the boundaries of the wood, who understood no other cries in the sky than those of the winds, and none on earth except the roaring of beasts, who had seen no other guests than his fellow woodsmen, now beheld how a strange glare blazed in the sky.

" 'A battle! Where? In what direction?' asked the young men as they seized their arms; the women raised their hands in prayer to Heaven. All, sure of victory, cried out with tears in their eyes: 'God is with Napoleon, and Napoleon is with us.' " *

Alas, their dreams of a restored Poland were not fulfilled.

But the singing still went on. The girls sang over their looms in Lowicz, where they wove cloth into adjacent stripes of color, just like the stripes of color in the Polish meadows where each different crop bears at ripening its own hue: "painted with grain, gilded with wheat, silvered

---

* From *Pan Tadeusz* by Adam Mickiewicz, translated by Prof. G. R. Noyes—Everyman Edition—Dutton, New York.

with rye; where grows the amber mustard, the buckwheat white as snow, where the clover glows with a maiden's blush, where all is girdled as with a ribbon by a strip of green turf."

They sang at Zakopane, up among the high Tatry Peaks, where the men wear long woolen trousers woven of goat hair, and heavily braided short coats, and a round mountaineer's hat. They sang in Chelmno, on the Vistula, where the stately Gothic buildings have looked down upon so much history. They sang in Lublin where the round tower of Jadwiga's castle arises above the grim fortress wall, and they sang far out on the steppe where the musicians still play a mandolin that operates from a wheel.

In the opera houses in the cities there was music and dance each night. At Krakow in the Slowacki Theater where Madame Modjeska, the famous actress, gave her farewell performance; at Warsaw, in the National Theater, where the boxes and loges were full of diplomats, men in uniforms, and women in the most gorgeous of evening gowns. They are fondest of a Polish opera, *Halka,* the story of a peasant girl in the Carpathians who may not marry the man of her choice because he is so far above her in social rank. But they love the foreign operas, even out in the coal fields of Dabrowa, and Sosnowiec, and Bedzin, and no war or suffering can prevent these from being shown. When Warsaw was besieged by the Russians in 1920, the government called for volunteers hastily, even when the city was being menaced—not men to fight, for everyone in the country had already volunteered for that—but men to play pianos and sing in public halls. And so, while the rolling guns were thundering through the streets, and the airplanes were drumming overhead, a great volume of song rose up everywhere in the city, for the audiences always arose and sang the choruses of all the songs that were sung on the stage.

Poland could not live without her music. In the churches the great chorales include majestic pieces like "From the Smoke of Dead Fires," or "God Preserve Poland." During Polish revolutions against powers that had conquered her, the Poles were forbidden to sing these songs in their own language. The conquerors thought that this had stopped the singing. But no—the congregations switched their words into Latin, and went on, regardless of the fact that soldiers stood at the door to mark the song leaders with chalk, and then single them out to send to foreign prisons.

And at Christmas! Then Poland gave over the whole country to rejoicing, and much of the rejoicing was in music. On Christmas Eve, four trumpeters mounted the high balcony of the Church of the Trumpeter, in Krakow, and played the little hymn "Amidst the Silence." High up on the walls the suspended organ pipes carried on the same melody, while in the body of the church and in the square outside, thousands of people stood, with uplifted heads, and sang:

> *"Through night's dark shadow*
> *Leaps the gladsome song;*

Shepherds acclaiming
Pass the news along
Haste, oh haste thee, Christ is living,
Bethlehem his cradle giving
Greet the new-born King."

For a whole week and more, clear up to the festival of the Three Kings, the celebration goes on. City streets are full of children with puppet shows, depicting the scenes at Christ's birth; halls are full of pageants; all the market-places are green with trees and brilliant with lights; in the houses great banquets are spread, and before the Christmas meal each partaker tastes first his neighbor's Christmas wafer. Out in the country, straw is placed beneath the wooden plates, and a vacant place is left at each table, in case the Christ Child should come in.

Modern trumpeter sounding the "Heynal."

The Polish spirit is the spirit of song, the song of sorrow, of courage. And that song which most typifies the Polish spirit is the little hymn called the Heynal, which is sounded hourly from the tower of the Church of Panna Marja, or the Church of the Trumpeter, in Krakow. Its sweet notes rise from a trumpet whose brass bell is clearly discernible from the street many hundreds of feet below. And at the end of the little strain is a sudden breaking off of the melody, in what Poles call the Broken Note.

"The Broken Note" Signal of the Trumpeter of Krakow

Now the story of this song and the Broken Note is known to many people throughout the world. It is the story of a youthful watchman who played a trumpet in this tower, when on duty there, when the Tartars were besieging the city, far back in the year 1241. He did not leave when the city was partly overrun, for he had taken an oath to stay on his post of duty, and he was shot through the body by a Tartar arrow which sped from a hostile bow below him. He was playing at the time he was shot, and he tried to finish the Heynal as he had sworn, but as his life ebbed slowly away, he sounded a last note, which was broken off when death overtook him. Therefore, from that day to this, the Krakow trumpeters have finished the Heynal on the Broken Note.

This story had a marvelous—I might say a miraculous —sequel in the year 1943, exactly seven hundred and two years later. A Polish historian who had been a prisoner in Russia, was released and on his way with other soldiers to the Allied bases in the Near East, when they happened to stop for the night in Samarkand.

There they were approached by the Imam from the Mosque of Mahomet that lay on the edge of the city. He was greatly excited.

That which follows is quoted from *Wiadomoscie Polskie,* a Polish newspaper published in London, the article in question being written by Ksawery Pruszynski.

"Are you from Lechistan?" asked the holy man.

"We are."

"And do you believe in God, your old God?"

"We do. We have priests; we carry the Cross."

"Have you trumpeters among you?"

"We have."

The Imam grew more and more excited. Finally he cried out: "Then will you do us a great favor. Will you have your trumpeters come to our Rynok (market-place) tomorrow evening and play in front of the Mosque, at the place where lies the tomb of the great Timur Khan?"

"What shall they play?"
place where lies the tomb of the great Timur Khan?"

"The sacred hymn that is played from the balcony of

the great church of your land every hour. I do not know its name—"

"Oh, that must be the Heynal," said one of the soldiers. "Yes, our trumpeters will gladly play it for you."

The Imam burst into tears and hurried away. Next evening the square was crowded with the inhabitants, all of them descendants of Tartars. Excitement was visible everywhere. Young and old fell on their knees before the four Polish trumpeters sent by their commander, kissing their hands and their coats. The trumpeters did not know what it was all about, but they advanced to the tomb of the great Tartar leader, and played the Heynal. After the first playing they were asked to play it again. They complied. Again. They played for the third time.

Then the scene became indescribable. The whole city went into a transport of joy. And the Imam, explaining, said to the Poles: "That removes the curse of our race. It happened seven hundred and two years ago that one of the warriors of the Tartars shot with a bow and killed a Lech (Polish) trumpeter while he was playing a sacred song. After that a curse fell upon our land. We were defeated in battle. We were enslaved. And an old prophet of that day said that the curse would never be taken away, until soldiers from Lechistan, believing in the old God, and bearing trumpets, should play the same tune before the grave of Timur Khan. Thus is the prophecy fulfilled. Samarkand's dark days are over, and a new era comes when the Tartars will become a free people, and will live like brothers with all nations ever after."

4

Polish People at Work and Play

Few countries of the world present a more striking picture of color and activity than Poland did before World War II.

When one entered the country then, by the port of Gdynia on the Baltic, one felt the stirring of a great national enterprise. Everything about was modern, the houses, wharves, ships, machinery. Out in the bay were the new Polish liners, the *Batory* and the *Pilsudski,* named after famous leaders, well equipped in every detail, plying between Poland, Belgium, France, England, and America.

The port itself is a miracle. When the old Polish port of Danzig was made a free city, in 1919, the German influences there were not friendly to Poland. So Poland built a huge canal running from the upper waters of the Vistula to the Baltic, and at the point where the canal entered the sea, arose the port of Gdynia. It was completed in less than twenty years, with American architects and engineers playing a great part, and by 1939 was the third Baltic port in importance of shipping.

From this hustling busy port, where one might see sailors from America, or England, or France, one descends the river to older towns and villages; and at once Poland is revealed, through the clothing and customs of her people, as a nation of great age.

Native costumes begin to appear, in the country, on the farms and even in city streets. Most generally among the farmer people, the women wear, on holiday occasion, the old *serduszek,* or embroidered vest, with skirts of many colors. There is much flaunting of ribbons, and at the neck are worn strings and strings of beads, "corale," or coral, sometimes as many as a dozen at a time, and in most cases they are family heirlooms. In the upper reaches of the Vistula in the country about Poznan, Torun, and Chelmno, the girls wear on festive occasions a long, combined vest and skirt-coat, white and laced, over a dark skirt. On the head, instead of the usual kerchief, is a large round, white hat, turban-shaped, caught with white lacy cloth at the chin, where over a great bowknot one sees a smiling and happy face.

Yet these girls do a man's work. One finds them in the fields in spring, summer, and fall, working alongside the

A typical Polish country scene, above, and girls celebrating the beginning of harvest in Swiebodzin.

men. Then, however, they are barefooted, hatless perhaps, except for a kerchief, in thick woolen dress, planting, weeding, or gathering up sheaves. With them are the boys, most of whom take care of the cows. One sees them at noon gathered about in a circle eating their lunch, and a very prominent American writer once said that he would give a good deal to know just what they were thinking about.

The girls work in the mines and factories as well. One finds them in the coal district at Dabrowa in the south, and in Silesia. On an early morning, in any of the larger cities, one sees them trooping gaily to work like the hat-girls in Paris.

They work hard, but there are some holidays—before the war there was almost one a week. Then one could see them carrying the banners in a parade to the church, or gathering in groups in the market-place and talking over the news—probably the news of their own village. Should a visitor go to a large market-place on any week day, he would have seen groups of girls waiting to be hired for work in some home, chattering spiritedly in the midst of all the cries of the market-place, the cackling of hens and geese, the grunting of pigs, the barking of dogs and the high voices of the farmers shouting their wares. The market is still a busy place, thronged with farmer people driving in from a distance in a wooden cart that rattles and bangs over every stone. The horse wears a great, high wooden collar, for just what purpose one can't see. Perhaps some five hundred years ago the carts were somehow

An old print of the Jewish market in Warsaw.

attached to this collar, but as years went on were improved and better secured; but customs are hard to change and the collar still lives. Amidst all these scenes, in a Polish city, there is the contrast of new and old. Automobiles speed by, airplanes drone overhead, troops of children go marching in modern costumes to their grammar or high school; new buildings, bridges, towers arise everywhere; but the horse still wears his five-hundred-year-old collar.

Following down the Vistula to Krakow and the Carpathians, one finds the people quite different in dress and customs, and sometimes even in the manner of speaking, but everywhere is the sparkle of animation and intelligence that marks the Polish people.

Before the war, on their national holiday, the 3rd of May, the anniversary of the adoption of their Constitution in 1793, the whole country would burst forth in an enthusiastic celebration. The Fourth of July was also celebrated, and on the 150th anniversary of our Independence Day, not only was a holiday proclaimed throughout Poland, but a great ceremony was held at the Kosciuszko Mound outside Krakow, when earth from Kosciuszko's battlefields in America—Yorktown, Saratoga, West Point —was added to the great mound, in a huge pageant of church, people, and soldiers.

In Krakow, Wilno, and Lublin—the last two cities ceded to Russia at the end of World War II—one could see before the war many of the black robes of the orthodox Jews. In the synagogues the rabbis read the sacred words of the scrolls of the Torah. In Lublin and in Wilno one found the old, dignified schools of training for rabbis, the men standing, their hats upon their heads, and their voices repeating those old, old words, that Christian and Jew know in so many languages, the words upon which so much of all religious belief is based. In old days, the Jews dwelt in the heart of each city, and often built walls about it so that it would be defended in time of war.

There were also many Jewish communities in the countryside. Neither these settlements nor the people can be seen today. Homes were razed and Jewish people killed by the Nazis during World War II.

The most famous costumes in Poland, perhaps, are the many-colored gowns of Lowicz, a famous center of weaving. Lowicz curtains, blankets, rugs, all in stripes of different colors, are now found on sale in all parts of the world. This town, which lies near the center of the country, has always been famous for its cloths, and the hand-weaving goes back many centuries. But the striking gay skirts and bodices of Krakow, centuries old in pattern, are perhaps the most colorful of all. One doesn't see so many of them at present as formerly, for the girls have seen American movies, and copy the dresses of the American stars of the screen.

But there is a festival on in Krakow. It is the day of Corpus Christi, the day when the Sacrament is borne outdoors into the square and the thousands there kneel reverently. The religious festival is hardly over, when there sounds a beating of drums and into the square dashes a man on a great hobby horse, carrying in his hands a whip to which are attached large soft balloon-like balls. With these he strikes out right and left, and the crowd, roaring and surging, tries to rush in on him, and strike at him, and

A peasant girl from Lowicz.

yet escape a beating. He is dressed like a Tartar, in rich eastern robe and huge turban, and he performs this wild rite every year in memory of the day when the Tartars took Krakow back in 1241. At the end of his trip, as a reward for the buffeting he has received, he is feasted by all the tradespeople. The man who performs this ceremony must be a direct descendant of one of the Poles who took part in the ancient battle.

There are many old customs which the Poles perpetuate. One is the throwing of water on girls on Easter Monday. The young ladies have a chance at the men later in the week. Then in the fall, images are made of straw and cast into the river, to float where they will and bring good

A students' festival.

luck to the sender. Some say that this commemorates the day when the Krakow girls threw flowers on the water, when Wanda floated down the river in her funeral barge. On the Eve of St. John the girls gather for a dance, and dream later of the men they are going to marry. Perhaps they even look in a mirror on that day to see if some young man is standing behind them. And out in the more lonely places, some still place food on the graves, on Forefathers' or All-Hallows' Eve, and many keep to their homes for fear of ghosts.

Through work and through play, life goes on. Christmas, Easter, the Saints' days—all are celebrated, but the great event of family life is the marriage of a daughter.

Celebrating the feast of Corpus Christi.

A peasant wedding in the Lowicz district.

Then the relatives all come, from miles about, to remain at the place of the marriage for a week or even more. The house is soon full to overflowing, and the late comers must sleep in the hay. There is everything under the sun to eat: beef and pork and mutton; cheeses in gorgeous shapes, beet-soup, cabbage, a great dish containing about everything called "bigos"; little sweet cakes topped with cream; chopped meat wrapped in a cabbage leaf and called a "dove"; crisp doughnuts (without the hole) all powdered over with sugar; dried fish, fancy breads, and last of all that delicious "lody"—a kind of ice cream which does not melt fast, but contains bits of cinnamon and citron and candies. A great day indeed is the wedding.

And even in the mines the work is not unmixed with pleasure. There are those great salt mines of Wieliczka

A chapel in the salt mines.

near Krakow, centuries and centuries old, where the men go down for hundreds and hundreds of feet through the old high tunnels, and rooms from which salt has been taken. In this very deep mine there is a lake, and the visitor can cross this lake in a boat, but he must be careful not to fall off, for the lake has no bottom. There are chapels and dance halls, with figures carved out of salt, and great chandeliers hanging from the roof encased in glittering salt crystals, so that when the light is turned on, the rooms sparkle with a dazzling brilliance. The horses that carry up the salt to the surface through long, winding tunnel shafts have worked in the dark for so many years that they are blind.

Those who live in the mountains have their own characteristic costumes. These are the Gorale people, in their white suits of goat hair, who have a language of their own and a history that is full of pride. They tell how they once saved a Polish king from defeat among their mountain passes. They say that when Poland was conquered they never gave in, but fought among the mountains until the end. This is where guerrilla units of Polish Resistance— the *Armija Krajowa,* or Polish Home Army—fought the Nazis in World War II, and where some of the embattled members of the Underground in the cities could find respite.

When a mountaineer dies, he is dressed in his best suit

A gorale boy of the Carpathian Mountains.

with the long, white, tight-fitting trousers, the richly embroidered vest and coat, and the round hat lined with
small shells. His casket is carried on the shoulders of his
friends to the nearest church. On the top of the casket is
laid his mountain axe, and the long coil of rope he had
worn at his belt when traveling the country of high and
dangerous peaks.

5

Krakow—the City of Kings

IN THE SOUTHWESTERN CORNER of Poland, where from its Wawel Hill one may look out to the distant Carpathian peaks; where one may glance eastward over hills and plains; where off to the north lies the winding valley of the Vistula, stands today the city of Krakow as it has stood for centuries and centuries.

As the most typical of Polish cities, as the center of Poland's greatness from the thirteenth to the sixteenth centuries, it holds within its heart many a Polish secret which it only reveals to those who really love it. The whole city has been described by visitors as one great museum, for one finds within it the work of hands and brains of countless thousands of painters, architects, sci-

Market Square in Krakow.

entists and merchants, and in its spirit lie the impulses of
the poet and the musician.

Around it flows the Vistula in a great curve; above it
rises the great Wawel Hill with its castle of the kings; off
on the horizon are the huge earthen mounds of the foun-
der Krakus and his daughter Wanda; and nearer at hand
is a similar mound to the leader Kosciuszko—famed in

Krakow's barbican, part of the town's fortifications.

both Poland and America—to which Poles from all over the world make a pilgrimage.

By the west gate, the gate of St. Florian, stands a huge red fortification or barbican, called the Rondel. It is one of the very few fortifications of this kind left in Europe. Men brought back patterns for these barbicans from the Crusades, and the French name, rondel, has curiously enough, in Polish, the meaning, "a frying-pan." Beyond this is a statue erected by Ignace Jan Paderewski, the musician and Premier, to Ladislaus Jagiello, the Lithuanian, and to the Poles and Lithuanians who followed him to battle against the Teutonic knights or Prussians in the year 1410. With that sense of humor characteristic of the Poles, there is a famous saying, or question: "Why is Ladislaus always hungry?" The answer is: "Because he is forever looking into the frying-pan, and yet can't help himself to anything in it."

Through the Florian Gate one comes to Florian Street, with its old buildings and Gothic designs. Here, in the first set of houses, once lived Joseph Conrad as a boy, when his father was an exile in Siberia, and down that street went the young Joseph every day on his way to the school which is now part of the University Library.

One might ask how Krakow preserves its old appearance, even to its private dwellings, and the answer is that the city has a law that no dwelling or building shall be taken down until it has become dangerous or unfit to live in, and if a new building is put up it must be exactly like the building that stood there.

Once—and until recently, too—there were walls about the whole city, walls with towers at short intervals, each manned in time of war by one of the trade guilds. Thus each tower bore a name: Carpenters' Tower, Woodworkers' Tower, Goldsmiths' Tower, and the like. Today the walls have been taken down, except for a stretch flanking the Florian Gate, and the sites they once occupied have been made into a continuous park, called the "planty" which encircles the whole city.

Through Florianska Street one comes to the Church of Our Lady, the Church of Panna Marja, the Church of the Trumpeter, for it is called by all three names. It rises majestically at one corner of the large open market-place called the Rynok, its two Gothic towers of unequal height facing the square. The story is that two brothers designed the church, but he who built the lower tower was angry that his brother had out-distanced him, and slew him with an old knife which still hangs from a chain in the Cloth Hall in the middle of the market-place.

This church is the pride of Poland. It embodies all that Poland means in fierce devotion to its faith, to patriotism, to beauty, to the quality of "everlasting" that Poland possesses. It is Gothic in pattern, of the Vistula variety, high, solid brick, with built-in buttresses at the base of each section. The so-called "flying-buttress" that one sees in western Europe is not found in Poland—perhaps because the built-in buttress stands the severe weather better.

From the high tower of the church, with its trumpeter's room and its outside circlet of little towers, a trumpeter, always on duty, sounds hourly to the four points of the compass the little hymn called the Heynal, or hymn with the broken note, in memory of the young trumpeter killed there by the Tartars more than seven hundred years ago. This little hymn has become, since 1939, a sacred symbol of the spirit of Poland, among Polish exiles all over the world.

The Church of Panna Marja in Krakow Square.

*A fragment of the Wyt Stwosz
altar in Panna Marja.*

Inside the church, with its high pointed arches, one
finds, among the vast store of artistic treasures, the great
altar piece, of wood-carving, depicting the death of the
Virgin. This altar piece, a most exquisite work, was finished by the wood-carver Wyt Stwosz in the later years
of the fifteenth century. The figures are life size, and are
so perfectly executed that they seem to be alive. Another
marvelous figure, in wood, is that of the Crucified Christ,
high in the nave. To all Poles, this church is a Mecca. It

stands on the site, perhaps on the foundations, of the old church burned by the Tartars in 1241.

Around this church still linger the memories and customs of the Poland of old days. There are the buildings housing the clergy who officiate in the services. There, beside a little court, one finds the remains of the old burying-ground. A grim reminder of medieval justice is the iron collar on a chain near one of the side doors to the church, where criminals were once secured as punishment for misdemeanors, by order of the city magistrates. Even this was a more merciful place than the pillory in the open square, for here the clergy and the faithful could minister to their relief.

The whole market-place, or *Rynok,* about the church is full of the memories of old days. In that house on the farther corner there was held in the sixteenth century the marriage feast of a man by the name of Dimitry and a girl, Marina, a daughter of the family living there. Now Dimitry claimed to be a long-lost son of Ivan the Terrible of Russia, and therefore heir to the Tsar's throne in Moscow. Immediately after the wedding feast he gathered together an army and marched on the Russian capital. Curiously enough, he was received with acclaim, and placed on the throne; but he did not occupy it long, for his pretense was soon discovered. He is known in history as the False Dimitry. In front of that remaining tower of the old town hall, the leader Kosciuszko, freshly returned from service with General Washington in the American Revolution, took a sacred oath that he would always serve the best interests of the Polish people. In that little chapel, seemingly ages old, St. Adalbert in early days preached to the people of Krakow, and along that side street the soldiers marched away with Sobieski to meet the invading Turks at Vienna.

Across the middle of the market-place stretches the Cloth Hall or Sukiennice. It seems like a rather low, much decorated structure with many pillars and Gothic arches, but it is really a thing of great beauty. As one discovers upon studying it, one whole story is now underground. It is a curious fact that cities rise with the course of years, with the result that, in entering most old Krakow buildings, one goes down a flight of stairs. Thus it is no unusual thing to find cellars of ordinary houses in Poland set on beautiful Gothic arches, for five hundred years ago the cellars were the first floors.

The Cloth Hall has been, in modern times, as busy as it was in 1462 when the market-place was thronged with merchants from all over the world. Horses, mules, camels, were all plentiful there. Armenian merchants had come in with carpets and rugs. Gypsies were there, as they are today, with bright-colored ribbons, offering to tell one's fortune. Greeks had come up from the south; Hanse merchants were there from Denmark, and the rich Hanse cities such as Lubeck. All tongues were spoken, all kinds of money passed hands; for Krakow lay upon the great trade routes which went from Europe to Asia, and the merchants were rich beyond the dreams of peasants or farm people.

The Cloth Hall.

Two gargoyles from the top of the Cloth Hall.

The great central portion of the buildings was once the cloth-market, where one purchased colored kerchiefs to wind about the head, tapestries, laces, embroidered vests for women—called *serduszeks*—skirts, aprons, ribbons. In addition one could find rare articles carved out of wood by the peasants—walking sticks, cut in the shape of axes, from the Carpathians; plates bearing mottos about the border, the most common of which was the old Polish saying, "A guest in the house is God in the house," or perhaps a line from the Lord's Prayer, or perhaps, "The hostess is merry when she has guests around her."

This Cloth Hall was once a plain Gothic structure, but in the sixteenth century, when King Sigismund married an Italian princess, she brought with her to Poland Italian architects who had adopted fashions in building which came in at about the same time as the discovery of America. This new type of architecture was very decorative, and the result is that the Cloth Hall bears a variety of stone figures over the old Gothic plainness—expressing the rich style of the Renaissance.

On the west balcony of this building, Prussian Duke Albert of Brandenburg swore on his knees loyalty to his sovereign, the King of Poland; but the years were to prove that the oath meant nothing, that Albert had only in mind the extension of the power of Prussia, to which he succeeded. A picture showing this scene was designed by the great Polish painter Matejko, whose life-long work among Polish historical subjects stamps him as a Polish Rembrandt.

Street after street leading from the square is rich with beautiful houses and Gothic doorways. But as one follows through one street, Golembia—the Street of the Pigeons—one passes by houses famous, of old, all over the world. This was once the street of magicians, the street of alchemists, who sought to turn iron and baser metals into gold. Here is reputed to have lived and studied that student, Faust, whose life Goethe studied before he wrote his famous play. A bronze tablet on a left-hand building at the corner of the square marks the residence of Goethe while he was studying. Certainly here lived the magician Twardowski, who escaped the Devil's clutches by flying over the city of Krakow on the back of a rooster.

At the end of this street is the beautiful building of the library, or Bibliotek, of the University. Once it was the housing place of doctors and masters. In its Gothic squareness and cloistered court, it is one of the most impressive buildings in Krakow. Copernicus, who in 1543 published his book *The Revolutions of the Heavenly Bodies,* once lived in or near this building. The University itself is the sixth oldest in Europe. It has always been noted for its astronomical studies, with two established chairs since 1390. Inside the building may be found treasures, books in vellum and old leather, a collection of ancient astronomical instruments, including an astrolabe that Copernicus probably used, and a globe of the earth from the year 1509, showing, for perhaps the first time in history, the newly named continent of America.

In that little chapel recess lived the venerable saint and scholar Jan Kanty, in the early years of the fifteenth century. So great a friend of students at the University was he, that it is no uncommon sight, at this day, to see a student, about to take an examination, drop on his knees for a second before his shrine, to ask him to make that examination a success.

And now one ascends the slope leading to the Wawel Hill, and the Castle of the Kings, with its Cathedral surrounded by small chapels built by successive kings, with its palaces graced by Italian doorways looking down upon pleasant courts. From this castle one can look off over the fields to the mountains, or one can look down upon the ancient spired city, as beautiful today as it was five hundred years ago. In the very building of the castle one can read the history of Poland. That curious little Gothic

An emblem of a crowned eagle carved in stone.

tower outbursting on the wall, with supports like long fingers, is called the Chicken's Foot, and there the loved Queen, Jadwiga, lived in 1386. Those walls and gates surround a grim space where malefactors were once punished—inside the old Cathedral the nobles assembled in prayer after their armies were beaten by the Tartars at the battle of Liegnica in the thirteenth century. Down be-

The Vasa and Sigismund chapels of the Wawel Hill Cathedral.

low the floors is the old crypt, Gothic in places, yet with older traces of earlier Romanesque, and here lie buried the great men of Poland—all the kings, the great general, Poniatowski, who perished at the battle of Leipsig under Napoleon, and Kosciuszko, who attempted to lead the Polish people to liberty and freedom.

Possibly Krakow began here—or perhaps on that other hill called Skalka. Were one to study and search this city through, for years, one would find new treasures every day.

6

As Warsaw Was

WARSAW! What magic is in the name. For many years this city stood for gaiety, color, intrigue, war, and romance. With its yellow buildings housing more than a million people up and down the banks of the ever-widening Vistula, it was in 1939 a city in which the modern age was rubbing shoulders with the memories of hundreds of years. Ten years later it was in ruins. But it has slowly been reborn.

Only a village of Mazowia when Krakow was already a great capital, it grew rapidly and steadily as traffic on the river increased by leaps and bounds. Then after the union of Poland and Lithuania, it became the meeting place of representatives from both countries, and after the discovery of America in 1492, when Krakow was no longer a great mart on the road to the east and trade, and attention was given to adventure and commerce in the west, Warsaw profited by her sister city's decline, and assumed an importance of her own.

By 1569 the parliaments of Lithuania and Poland were meeting in Warsaw. In 1572 the election of the Polish rulers began there. In 1595 Sigismund the Third of the Swedish House of Vasa moved the capital, bag and baggage, from the southern city, and from that time Warsaw became the chief city of the realm.

There are but a few relics left of the very ancient Warsaw, though here and there about the town old remnants of the first walls have been discovered recently and rebuilt. Yet as Warsaw came into the company of capital cities of Europe, the day of old fortified castles on hills was about over. Men were now making war with firearms. Artillery and muskets, clumsy at first, grew more and more important as years went on, so that a city which was "spread out" suffered less during a siege, and could be defended better, than a castled city, which was smaller and circumscribed by walls.

The Old Warsaw lies upon a slight elevation above the river. Here once one found in the old market-place a long line of highly colored buildings unlike anything elsewhere. The most noteworthy of these houses, a famous wineshop,

A painting by Canaletto of Miodowa Street in Warsaw towards the end of the eighteenth century.

had been a center of informal gatherings since 1590. One hopes that this building, damaged as it was, may be rebuilt. But the Palace of the Kings, which lay at the edge of the old city, and which, in long yellow lines, ran down to the river, is a mass of ruins. This Palace was the scene of the hilarious gaiety of the late seventeenth century when Stanislaus Augustus was king, and the country was trembling on the brink of ruin. Close by the Palace was the stately Warsaw Cathedral, with high Gothic arches. It was designed and begun in the fifteenth century by the house of Mazowia, but reconstructed and renewed in the nineteenth. Alas, it is all gone now.

Just down the street there was an old hotel, the English Hotel, or to give it the name it bore, L'Hôtel d'Angleterre. Outside, it appeared like any other hotel in Warsaw, but inside one marked the great array of red plush in chairs and sofas, bearing the royal crown of an emperor. There is an amusing story told about this once famous hotel.

In the bitter cold winter of 1812–13, there returned to Warsaw the same Napoleon who had left it in triumph but a short time before. Then he was a conqueror with the world at his feet. Now he was a badly defeated general returning from a campaign in Russia in which he had seen his splendid army almost wholly destroyed in a terrible winter of fighting.

As he entered the street on which the hotel stood, a courier handed him a message. It read, "England has declared war upon you."

Napoleon said nothing, but looked about for a place to

stay. The city had a bleak, deserted look; windows were barred and all doors were closed. Evidently news of the defeat of the French armies had reached Warsaw.

Suddenly he saw the sign "Hotel." Quickly he rushed up to it and saw that the door was partly open. "At last," he said, "we have a place to stay."

But then he looked at the sign again, and read the whole lettering upon it . . . "The English Hotel," it said.

The Emperor hesitated, thinking of the news the courier had brought him. Had Fate laughingly brought him to this place?

Then he shrugged his shoulders. He was cold and hungry. "Any port in a storm," he exclaimed, and went inside.

From this point the city spread out along the river, full of gorgeous buildings such as the Grand Opera House, St. Anne's Church, and the National Museum. One traversed the Saxon Gardens which bordered the palace of the Saxon kings, one passed by the splendid memorial to the Unknown Soldier of the First World War, and came by the Street of the New World to the long avenue or Aleja where were broad parks and fine residences. At the very end, in a beautiful setting, was the Lazienki Palace of Stanislaus Augustus, the last king of Poland. Adjoining it was an open air theater, designed like the ruin of an ancient classic courtyard, with one arm of a little lake flowing in between the audience and the stage. As memories of the palace and its luxury, its regal bed-chamber with classic paintings, its Green Chamber with the portraits of the most beautiful women of Poland, its rotunda

An old house in Warsaw, destroyed in World War II.

The eighteenth century Lazienski Palace, the summer residence of King Stanislaus Augustus in Warsaw, destroyed in World War II.

with statues of all the kings of Poland—as these memories are held in the mind, so come pictures of the luxury and splendor of the parties which were held in the park, the performances in the little theater, the pageants which the nobles of the eighteenth century so much loved. These, too, are gone.

And no one loved pageants more than the Poles. Whole fortunes were spent sometimes on a single entertainment. When a king once visited a noble in the country, that noble transformed his whole estate into a scene from classical Greek mythology. Various gods and goddesses welcomed the royal guest, a raft load of beautiful shepherd-girls in high, powdered wigs and fluffy silk robes —such as no shepherdess could ever have afforded— floated on a little lake on a gilded barge bearing the figure of Neptune on the prow. Cattle were slaughtered galore, wine-cellars were emptied, cakes and dainties were produced by the thousand. Certainly the poor nobleman must have been reduced to bread and water for years after the royal visit.

Warsaw became in the twentieth century a great business mart, a city of factories, shops, and office buildings, extending along side streets for miles. Then there are the government buildings—the Belvedere Palace where the president of the country made his home, the foreign offices and the buildings of the foreign legations. Outside the city is to be found a rare gem, the old palace of Jan Sobieski who held off the Turks from Poland and finally from all Europe in the battle of Vienna in 1685. This is called Wil-

A detail from the twelfth century bronze portal of the Cathedral of Gniezno, province of Poznan, showing the slaying of St. Adalbert.

lanow and contains some priceless works of art, some tapestries taken from the Turks after Vienna, sculpture, seventeenth-century furniture—all rich, in the Baroque fashion.

Then hasten down the river in a little steamer, to transfer later to rail, and one is in Czestochowa, the sacred city of Poland. Above the town on a hill rises the Bright Mountain, surmounted by a walled cloister, with the spire of one church rising high above the other buildings. In this church is a spacious chapel housing in its shrine the Miraculous Image or Picture of the Virgin, to which Poles by the hundreds of thousands have been accustomed to make pilgrimages every year. The painting itself is dark, set in gold, with a gold crown, and mounted on a silver altar, the gift of a noted chancellor in the seventeenth century. Reproductions of this picture are found all over Poland. It is truly the most beloved of the Polish Madonnas.

And this monastery has a vivid history. When the Swedes poured into Poland in the sixteenth century they were surprised to find little opposition. However, when they reached Czestochowa and tried to take the monastery, the Poles living there put up a very determined resistance. In a night it seemed, since now the most sacred shrine in Poland was in danger, the Polish people rose up *en masse* and drove the Swedes out. The novelist Henryk Sienkiewicz has a very fine account of it in his novel *The Deluge*.

Farther to the north is the old capital city of Poznan, where but little remains of the glory of the ancient days, except the magnificent Cathedral with its doors of bronze, and the old town hall with its exquisite council chamber. Poznan is also the home of a university located in what had once been a palace of the Hohenzollerns when they ruled over a conquered Poland. Poznan's neighbor, Torun, the birthplace of Nicholas Copernicus, boasts some magnificent churches and a very fine town hall the construction of which was begun in the year 1259. Along the Vistula in this region—the province of Pomorze— lie some very old Gothic cities such as Chelmno, Chelmza, and Bydgosc.

But there is another part of Poland, a very ancient part too, which lies far to the east through the fertile lands of Galicia, a province named from an old city that was once the capital, the city of Galich, which was destroyed by the Tartars in the early years of the thirteenth century. The capital is now the Russian city of Lwow, which takes its name from an ancient ruler and his family, Duke Lev, meaning the Lion, the city's name implying, thereby, the City of the Lions, marked by two statued lions which recline on stone at the entrance to the city building.

An old country this is, a country of war and struggle and suffering. In early days the road to it from the east, across the steppes or prairies, was called the Black Trail, significant of the dark deeds that were performed there. The early Pole or Lech fought there with the dukes of the Russian Kiev, and along its hard course came the Hungarians into Europe, followed by the Huns, the Tartars, and the Turks. Every inch of the road has been at some time soaked with blood. The very chapels out in the country contain vaults that are white with the bones of victims. On every hill through Wolynia and Podolia, the adjoining provinces, rise the ruins of high castles that have been destroyed by invaders from the east.

Yet Lwow is a beautiful and a very religious city. For here are the seats of the bishops of three churches, the Roman Catholic, the Orthodox, and the Armenian. As Lwow has an oriental touch, one finds here some eastern treasures, Armenian designs and works of art, Ruthenian embroideries, Russian ikons.

From a hill where once lived the ancient dukes, the city straggles down into a plain. There once were walls here, too, but with time the walls have fallen into decay. People of all races and creeds throng the streets; the stores have boasted fine jewels and precious stones; the old trade of the silversmith still continues, and a great fair, held each fall until 1939, brought purchasers and buyers from east and west together. Poland fought hard for centuries to defend this land against Asiatic invasion. She established a university here, built schools and museums containing the relics of the days of Sobieski and his warriors. In modern days, Lwow has become a great railroad center and has some notable industries, and her people are the same as in old days, Poles and Ruthenians. In 1946 it was annexed to Russia.

Beyond the northeast boundary, in the USSR, now with its old Lithuanian name of Vilnyus, is the city which the Poles call Wilno. It became part of the Polish Commonwealth when Duke Ladislaus Jagiello married Queen Jadwiga. There is so much in common between the Pole and the Lithuanian, and so much mixture of blood through intermarriage, that when the Polish poet Mickiewicz wrote his great national poem, *Pan Tadeusz,* he began it: "Lithuania, my country, thou art like unto health; one never knows its worth until one loses it." And Mickiewicz was writing a poem about Poland.

To Pole and Lithuanian, Wilno is so dear that it is hoped that in the future both will be in peaceful occupation of it as they had been for so many centuries. In Wilno

arose the great Polish school of revolution against Russia, students of the University leading the uprising. And from them came the great ideas that enlivened Polish minds and gave hope, during all the long years of Poland's captivity. King Stefan Batory of Poland in the sixteenth century founded a university in Wilno which was famous throughout the east.

But that for which Wilno is perhaps best known is the Madonna of the Ostra Brama, a lovely portrait of the Virgin which hangs above the main gate by which one enters the city. To it, as to Czestochowa, pilgrims flock by thousands in the months of spring, summer, and early fall, bearing their treasures to the beloved shrine, and praying for and receiving health. The chapel which holds the picture of the Madonna is located directly above the great arch on the inner side of the wall.

All around the city are thick forests and winding streams, teeming with folk-lore tales of the ancient Lithuanians. From a distance it really seems as if the city had grown up in the very middle of the woods, with the hill where once lived the Lithuanian dukes still bearing the ruined tower of the chieftain, Gedymin. Below it is a stately cathedral, white-pillared and square, standing upon the very place where, according to tradition, once stood a temple to Perun, God of Thunder. Off to the right is an architectural gem, a late-Gothic edifice, the Church of

The Ostra Brama Gate in Wilno.

The tower or back entrance to a seventeenth century wooden church in the Gothic tradition in the province of Krakow.

A farm near Poznan.

St. Anne, so striking in appearance and so rhythmical in its lines that Napoleon, on a visit to Wilno, declared that he wished some day to transport it to Paris.

There are many other cities in Poland, all possessing scenes of interest and beauty, like the Krakow Gate in the old city of Lublin, or the town hall in the city of Kazimir, built almost wholly by one king. There are scenes of delight in the mountains, old wooden churches and curious, artistically carven shrines. In fact, there is hardly an inch of Poland that does not possess some interest to the historian or the chronicler or the seeker for beauty; but it would take one man's lifetime to seek out the most interesting spots in just one such city as Krakow.

7

Poland's Honor Roll

A COUNTRY IS KNOWN for its great men and women. One could no more think of America without Washington or Lincoln or Franklin than one could think of France without Joan of Arc, or England without Wellington or Shakespeare.

And so with Poland. In her thousand years of existence as a nation, there have been at all times men and women of talent and genius who have thrown the brilliance of their careers against a national mirror, and the light has illumined not only Poland but all Europe, and in certain cases the whole world.

There went up to the University of Krakow in the year 1491 a youth of medium stature, dark hair, with long tapering agile fingers that immediately suggested an artist of exactness. This youth bore the name Copernik, but when he came to the University they gave him a Latin name, Copernicus, as was the case with all students, and arranged his studies at his own request so that he would be with Professor Adalbert of Brudzewo, the foremost astronomer of his time.

Krakow's skies are very clear. From the observatories in that city many valuable additions to astronomy have been made. And in later years the coming of many new comets have been first noted there.

Copernicus fell under the influence of this University, which in the Middle Ages excelled in the study of astronomy. The teaching which he received was largely mixed with philosophy and speculation, but he applied to astronomy the principles of mathematics and also the principles of experimental science, something that had not been done before. When he left the University he was convinced that something was wrong with men's beliefs about the earth and the heavens.

So he went on to Italian universities to try to solve the problem: Does the sun revolve about the earth or the earth around the sun? The world believed that the sun revolved around the earth, that the earth stood still in space as the very center of the universe. But Copernicus applied geometry and trigonometry to that theory. He drew circles on a chart showing the course of the planets in the sky.

Now he found that these were not perfect circles. And

Students at the University of Krakow.

anything that is not perfect, to the real mathematician is as hurtful to his mind as a discordant note is to a musician.

Finally in 1543 he put forward his theory in a book, *The Revolutions of the Heavenly Bodies*. For some fifty years he had worked on the idea of the earth turning on its own axis and sweeping about the sun in a large circle. Although he was convinced of this truth many years earlier, he did not wish to publish the theory until it was perfectly worked out.

Since all men had believed that the earth stood still and the sun revolved about it, such an idea was so shocking that it took the world two hundred years to grasp it fully. However, today all our ideas of the planets and space are based on the theory of Copernicus. Copernicus died the same year that his book was published, but he did at least have a chance to see it.

Poland's honor roll contains the names of the Polish generals who took part in the American Revolution and fought for liberty. One of these was Thaddeus Kosciuszko. Another distinguished general was Casimir Pulaski, who fought and died on American soil.

A few years before the American Revolution, Count Pulaski took part in an insurrection against Poland's last king, Stanislaus Augustus Poniatowski. The insurrection was defeated, and Casimir Pulaski was forced to flee abroad. At last he found refuge in Paris, where he met Benjamin Franklin in 1776. Franklin helped Pulaski to reach the American shore in 1777 and join George Washington's army.

Pulaski fought with distinction in many battles. A trained soldier, he commanded units of American cavalry and in the battle of Brandywine fought so skillfully and bravely that the Congress promoted him to the rank of brigadier general. Pulaski fought at Valley Forge and after that terrible winter, he was allowed by the Congress to form an independent corps of cavalry and light infantry which became known as the Pulaski Legion. In 1779, during the siege of Savannah, Georgia, Casimir Pulaski was mortally wounded. He died aboard one of the first ships of the American Navy, the *Wasp,* which was moored off Savannah. His bravery and death forged the early ties of friendship between the United States and Poland.

But these ties were not of a military nature alone. The many thousands of Polish families which immigrated to America in the course of history helped the nation's development. Some of the immigrants made significant contributions to the arts. One of them was the actress Helena Modjeska. Although well known on the stage in Warsaw, she left her oppressed land in the late nineteenth century and came to America as an immigrant. After a while, and with great effort, she mastered the English language so well that she made her way to the stage in New York. As she had become an American, America shares with Poland the glory of Modjeska's career.

There are some people who think that musicians are impractical. Perhaps Ignace Jan Paderewski, who died in 1942, is an exception. From being one of the most distinguished musicians and composers in the world, he evolved into a statesman and diplomat, to hold the highest position of power in the new Poland that was created after World War I. All his life, Mr. Paderewski had made a great deal of money from his concerts, but practically all of this money went into the Polish cause. It was he who was called into a conference with Colonel House and President Wilson, to help re-establish Poland in 1917; and after the conference he threw all his influence behind the new Polish government, in which he was Premier later.

His money helped to finance an army—the Haller

Ignace Paderewski.

Army which fought with the Allies in France. This same army went to Poland after the war and helped establish peace there. For when Poland first became a nation again in 1918, it was in terrible condition. Three armies had swept across it, destroying crops and livestock, and taking away not only its food, but even the blankets and pillows from the beds. The bells in the churches had been stolen and melted down for ammunition by the Germans.

So when Mr. Paderewski arrived in Warsaw in that year, a huge crowd of hungry people came marching up to his hotel demanding food. They were in such condition that they were capable of doing almost anything. An attempt was made by some nervous officials to remove Mr. Paderewski from the hotel by the back door, but he refused. Instead, he walked deliberately into the midst of the none too friendly crowd, and raising his voice, talked for more than an hour. He told them what he was doing, how relief supplies were on the way, how order would be restored everywhere, and at the end the crowd cheered him. That very day the first of the relief trains began to arrive, and Polish people needed no longer to eat bread made half of flour and half of sawdust.

It is now possible to read in English a translation of the great national poem of Poland—*Mr. Thaddeus*—or *Pan Tadeusz,* as the Polish title goes. It was written by a young man who had been one of a group of Polish revolutionists in the University of Wilno, in the late 1820's. Forced to flee the country because of his writings, he went to Paris, where he taught in the Sorbonne, and under a terrible depression, caused by homesickness, he wrote the poem which has been the comforting hope of Poles all over the world. It is the story of a young Polish student, who comes back to his home in the country south of Wilno to find everything in disorder because of the war between France and Russia.

It is a stirring romance, a fine story, and well worth reading, and its descriptions of life on an old Polish country estate, and the people who live there, are unsurpassed. He describes their food and feasting: a fish that was baked at the head, boiled at the tail, and fried in the middle, and yet served whole and on one dish; a scene in ice cream on a huge table showing the Polish parliament, a snow storm, and figures of men and women during the four seasons of the year. He tells of the glories of the hunt, the mysteries of the Lithuanian forests, describes in stirring fashion the playing of Jankiel, the Jewish tavern-keeper, upon a dulcimer, and at the end, tells of the coming of Napoleon. It is glorious and stirring.

Henryk Sienkiewicz, the great Polish novelist, author of *Quo Vadis* and *The Polish Trilogy,* tells a story of a lighthouse-keeper in Panama whose job it was to fill and light the beacon each day. One day a ship came near and tossed some books to the keeper. One of these books was *Pan Tadeusz,* and the lighthouse-keeper, being a Pole, seized the book and began to read. He read all day and he read all night, and in the morning when the government boat appeared, its angry officials demanding to know why the beacon hadn't been lighted, they found the Polish exile, with tears streaming down his face, still reading the poem with its scenes of his native land.

When the First World War was declared in 1914, there was, wandering about in the old library of the University of Krakow, a very distinguished man, Joseph Conrad. He had been away from his native land for many years, had traversed all the seas of the globe as an English sailor, had won fame as an English novelist. But his whole life was centered upon one thing, the freeing of his own country from its conquerors. He tells, himself, how he came out of the dark quiet shades of that old medieval library with its memories of great chroniclers and men of learning, blinded a little by the late afternoon sun reflected from old Krakow walls. As he reached the street he heard newsboys shouting, "War is declared! War is declared!" He reached eagerly for a paper, read the news briefly, and then breathed to himself, "Has it come at last? Has it come at last?" He was thinking of the deliverance of his country from Austria and Russia and Germany.

Throughout time, the Polish nation has given the world many remarkable figures. There are women like Queen Jadwiga who in the fourteenth century accomplished union between Poland and Lithuania, and the conversion of the Lithuanians to Christianity, without bloodshed, in an age when violence and bloodshed were prevalent, and like Mme. Marie Sklodowska Curie, who made possible the understanding of radiation in the twentieth century. Then there are artists like the composer Chopin and the novelist Sienkiewicz, men of the turbulent nineteenth century whose works are appreciated throughout the world today. In Poland reborn after World War I, the novelist Reymont won the Nobel Prize for Literature in 1924; and Joseph Conrad's writing, mostly in English, lives on.

The bitter years of World War II and the period which followed threw dark shadows which obscured for a while but did not destroy the ancient Polish culture. Toward the end of 1956, as the Poles forced the Communists to respond to popular demands for greater cultural freedom, along with other important political changes, the nation's hopes for its future revived and the Polish arts suddenly burst into a long-awaited flowering. In painting and sculpture, literature and theater and motion pictures as well, Poland was flooded with a wide range of creative works, after many years cut off from cultural contacts and exchanges with the world.

A harbinger of this development was the writer Adam Wazyk, whose "Poem for Adults" was published in 1955. In it Wazyk spoke out frankly and forcefully against the poverty, brutality, and injustice which had befallen his proud land under the new system. Then, there was the novelist Marek Hlaszko, whose stories about the stark life of the Poles won him worldwide fame. After the political changes in late 1956, Wazyk and Hlaszko were followed by a great many other authors. Most of them were thought of as belonging to a "pessimist" school of literature; and while they do in fact reflect strong pessimism in describing conditions in Poland, most of their work also shows much hope for the future of their country. Others in this movement were the novelist Jerzy Putrament, who lashed out at thinly disguised and easily recognizable characters— who were Poland's Communist leaders—in his novel, *Those of Little Faith;* Adam Augustyn, who in his novel *The Pagan* wrote openly about the Poles' indifference and disdain for the system which was not one of their choice; and Eugenusz Kabatz, who expressed the anger of the younger generation in his novel, *The Turtles.*

Some authors, of course, took an opposite view of life in Poland and called for strict controls of the arts, as Jerzy Jesionowski did in his story, *Twenty Lashes.* Nevertheless, throughout the 1960's and into the 1970's, Polish literature continued to flower, and new authors, too many to mention, appeared on the literary stage. Poland remains a nation of readers—just one of the many publishing houses in Poland, *Kiazka i Wiedza* ("Book and Knowledge"), published in twenty-five postwar years some thirty thousand works and distributed nearly three hundred million books—an impressive volume of reading for a nation of thirty-two million people.

Along with books, theater has always been very important in Poland as a form of literary expression. Since 1956, Polish theater has expanded its range from classical drama into modern and experimental productions. Student theaters surprisingly professional in quality sprang up throughout Poland, presenting both Polish and Western plays, classical as well as avant-garde, while the Polish National Theater and the Classical Theater of Warsaw received the finest notices when they toured abroad. No Polish theater, however, received as splendid notices as the Polish Laboratory Theater of Wroclaw. The acting method of its actor-director Jerzy Grotowski was described in the United States in 1969 as "perhaps the most influential in the Western Hemisphere."

The stifling but obligatory "socialist realism" of postwar painting and sculpture was replaced by the modern abstract work of Henryk Stazewski and many other painters and sculptors. Their works received fine notices time and again as they were shown in Europe and the United States. Polish motion pictures, with their stark realism and passionate concern for man's condition, gave the world many young directors—and an intimate glimpse, visual as well as verbal, into Poland reborn and holding great cultural promise.

8

Poland Embattled

POLAND, lying as it does upon the border of western civilization, has been a powerful barrier against the invasion of the West by eastern nations. Some thirty times invading hordes of Mongols threw themselves at that barrier and were driven back, at enormous cost of human lives and property. Time and again Polish forces stopped Turkish advances into central Europe. The most important of these was of course the Turkish campaign in the late seventeenth century which ended at Vienna when Jan Sobieski, king of Poland, defeated the Turks well on their way to invade Germany and France.

The rise of neighboring countries, and especially Russia, led to repeated invasions of Poland in the late seven-

105

teenth and eighteenth centuries. Sweden, Prussia, Russia
and Austria invaded Poland, making it a vast battlefield.
Time and again Poland rallied its forces to drive away the
conqueror, but in 1795 the end came as Polish independence was lost and the land partitioned between Russia,
Prussia, and Austria. Throughout the nineteenth century
the Poles struggled to recover their freedom. At the end
of World War I Poland's regions were reunited. Foreign
fetters were shaken off and the nation's independence restored. However, almost immediately, Poland was invaded by the Russians who advanced to the gates of
Warsaw in the summer of 1920. They were driven back
by the Poles.

An uneasy peace reigned in Poland for nearly twenty
years, while two giants—Soviet Russia in the east and
Hitler's Germany in the west—gathered strength. World
War II began with Germany's attack on Poland.

If you lived in Poland in 1939, you would have looked
about you with fear and apprehension. And, almost without hope. For, in the east was the mighty Russia with its
millions of people, its vast army, its unlimited resources.
In the west was a Germany dominated by Hitler, whose
dream of world conquest was on the way to realization.
England and France were seemingly powerless, having
already sacrificed Czechoslovakia and Austria to the conqueror without a battle. America seemed unconcerned,
striving for the most part to keep out of all European com-
plications.

German scientists were working on "secret weapons,"

flying bombs and rockets, poison gases and nuclear weapons. In five years, as it is now estimated, these weapons would have been perfected and the world would have been at Hitler's mercy. However, Hitler was the impatient type. Conquest had been so easy in the Ruhr, in Austria and in Czechoslovakia. Western diplomats with the motto "Peace in Our Time" were delaying and appeasing as each new issue came up. Although the new "secret weapons" had not quite been completed, Hitler decided to move eastward. He had unchallenged superiority in the air and on the land.

With the world asleep, or striving desperately to keep an impossible peace at any price, the next move was simple. In late August 1939 Germany concluded a treaty of friendship with Russia. This offset Poland's mutual non-aggression pact with Russia. Polish treaties with England and France guaranteeing her borders were believed by Hitler to be ineffective, since similar treaties had not been honored when Germany conquered Czechoslovakia.

A week after the pact with Russia was signed, Germany launched a powerful attack on Poland. Thus, on September 1, 1939, World War II began. However, the war was not limited to Poland alone because two days later England and France, honoring their treaties, came to Poland's aid and declared war on Germany.

Germany launched overwhelming forces against Poland. While bombs rained on Warsaw day and night, German infantry and armor seized the harbor of Gdynia, the miracle port on the Baltic. Penetrating deep into southern

Poland, the Germans seized the Shrine of Czestochowa—
the center of Polish religious life—and moved into the
historical city of Krakow, abandoned by the Poles in order to save its historic buildings. Then the invading
armies laid siege to Warsaw. Continuous bombardment
destroyed large sections of the capital, and such ancient
historic buildings as the Kraszinski Library, the Warsaw
art museum, the palace of the Saxon kings, and many
others went down in rubble.

But the Poles fought back. Guns were dragged to the
outskirts of Warsaw by men, women, girls and boys, and
units hastily composed of civilians helping the outnumbered Polish armies. The whole city rose up overnight,

Digging trenches in Warsaw at the outbreak of World War II.

lined the streets with barriers to impede the advance of tanks, dug trenches, removed top planking from all bridges, manned disused pillboxes in the suburbs and mounted machine guns. Some 60,000 men, women and children died in the defense of Warsaw.

At this moment, seventeen days after the outbreak of war, Russia entered the picture, and its troops entered Poland from the east. Their work was really simple. They broke upon a people fleeing one enemy and trying to make some organization against that enemy. All the Russians had to do was to gather the fugitives by the thousands, seize helpless cities and begin mass deportations to Russia and the Siberian prison camps. Attacked from two sides, Poland fell. Its government fled abroad to set up eventually the Polish government-in-exile in London. Thousands of Poles managed to flee through Rumania and by round-about routes to France and England where they formed Polish armies. These would fight alongside the Western Allies against Germany throughout the war. Polish air force squadrons bombed Germany, while infantry and armored units fought on all fronts.

Poland was divided between Germany and Russia. Hundreds of thousands of Polish soldiers were taken prisoner of war and shipped off to camps in Germany or Russia. In the German occupation zone the large Polish-Jewish population was marked for destruction. In the Russian zone, the policy was to destroy the educated and the more prominent Poles in order to render the nation leaderless.

Over 10,000 officers captured by the Russians and held in the Katyn camp in eastern Poland were executed. They were mainly reserve officers—physicians, engineers, lawyers, teachers and scientists—who had left their professions to defend Poland. Other officers and soldiers were deported to Russian slave labor camps and denied their right to treatment as prisoners of war. Tens of thousands of boys and girls, in their 'teens or twenties, were also deported to the camps although they had not been in the armed service. Thousands of families were taken from their homes and resettled in Russian villages. Before long these families got in touch with each other. It is said that if a Pole managed to escape from a Siberian camp and reach one of the resettled families, he would be secretly passed on to the family in the next village, and so on until he returned to Poland via this "underground railroad."

In the German zone of occupation the Jewish people were executed in large numbers and the rest of the Polish people were marked for servitude. In the Nazi scheme of things, they were to be denied education and would forever remain slaves of the Germans. But in the occupied villages and cities of Poland people began organizing underground resistance to the Germans. Bands of armed guerrillas roamed the deep forests and grew in size as people fleeing German persecutions joined them.

The German-Russian friendship and joint occupation of Poland ended abruptly in June 1941, as Germany launched an attack on Russia, her former ally, advancing deep into the Russian land and seizing hundreds of thou-

Jews being marched from the Warsaw ghetto to concentration camp transportation.

sands of war prisoners. Poland became the important strategic area in the rear of the German front in Russia, as all supplies for the German armies had to pass through it. Polish resistance engaged itself in sabotage, blowing up railroad lines, bridges, and German depots. This brought even harsher reprisals upon the Polish people.

Although both Poland and Russia were fighting the same enemy, the Russians still held the Polish prisoners and refused to recognize the Polish government-in-exile as Poland's lawful government.

Meanwhile the Germans made Poland into the execution place where not only Polish Jews but all Jews from the conquered countries, were brought to die. At first, in 1939, 1940 and 1941, German special units carried out mass executions of the Jews on the spot. They would round up entire Jewish towns or villages, machine-gun men, women and children, and set fire to the buildings. Later on, infamous death camps were built, such as Auschwitz, near the Polish town of Oswiecim, and many others. Long trains overflowing with wretched human beings—Jewish families and other people captured by the Germans in the conquered countries—arrived every day at the camps. Prisoners were herded by the hundreds into gas chambers and killed. The bodies were then burned to ashes in camp crematoriums so that no trace of the hideous crimes would be left. Week after week, month after month, year in and year out the dense acrid smoke of the crematorium chimneys crawled over the Polish land.

Over 50,000 Polish Jews had been herded by the Germans into the Warsaw ghetto, an old section of the city which was then surrounded by a wall. There they awaited transportation to the death camps. In April 1943, the people of the Warsaw ghetto rose in rebellion. They had neither arms nor supplies. Germany was at the peak of its power, and the Jews of the ghetto had no hope of winning or surviving the battle. Still they rose, preferring to die in battle rather than be led to slaughter. They fought with home-made weapons, with paving stones and bricks, with knives and kitchen utensils, against tanks and aircraft, heavy artillery and quick-firing automatic weapons of the infantry. All fought—men and women, the very young and the very old, the sick and the wounded—and virtually all died. They fought from mid-April to mid-May, and when the month was over, over 56,000 people lay in the smoking ruins of the ghetto. Those who still breathed, the ill, the wounded and the infants, were shot on the spot by the Germans. Only five or six survived, by miracle.

Russia was in mortal danger from the Germans and was willing to make concessions in return for all the west-

All that remains of the Warsaw ghetto: rubble and a Catholic church.

ern aid it could obtain. In 1942 Russia recognized the Polish government-in-exile and agreed to release Polish prisoners. Since they could not return to their German-occupied homeland, the ex-prisoners were allowed to leave Russia for the Near East. In Persia, in Egypt and in North Africa, the tens of thousands of Polish prisoners coming from Russia were formed into new armies. They fought alongside the Allies until the Germans and Italians were dislodged from Africa. Together with the American and British armies they landed in Italy in 1943 and fought with valor and distinction. Many died there with the name of Poland on their lips, and all dreamed of the day when the war would end in victory and they would return home.

Aircraft of the British-based Polish air force occasionally made the arduous flight from England over Germany to parachute supplies to the guerrillas in Poland. Polish resistance forces persisted throughout the entire land, continuing to sabotage German army installations, fighting pitched battles with the enemy and radioing intelligence to Allied headquarters in London. The Germans were withdrawing from Russia which, by 1944, was cleared of them (except for hundreds of thousands of war prisoners). In August of that year, large Russian forces stood at the gates of Warsaw as the Germans made ready to flee the capital.

In the city of Lublin in southeastern Poland, then under Russian control, a committee had been set up with the aim of replacing the Polish government-in-exile (then still in London) and setting up in its stead a communist sys-

tem in Poland. Polish underground resistance, still loyal
to the government-in-exile, attempted to offset this plan.
They hoped to force the Germans out of the nation's capital and to make possible the lawful government's return
from London to Warsaw.

Therefore, in early August 1944, the people of Warsaw rose up against the Germans. Deadly battles were
fought in the streets and parks, within the buildings and
on the rooftops, and even in the sewers under the city.
Several districts were liberated and held against assaults
of German tanks and bombardment by heavy artillery
and aircraft. These heroic insurgents had mistakenly believed that while they fought the German forces, the Russians would also move forward and help liberate the
entire city, but as the battle wore on and German rein-
forcements poured into Warsaw, days and then weeks
passed while the Russian armies stood still in sight of the
agonized city.

The insurgents grew short of food, medical supplies,
and ammunition. Outnumbered, they radioed desperate
appeals to the Polish government in London and to the
Allied powers asking for help. The Allies implored the
Russians to move forward and relieve Warsaw, but the
Russians remained still and silent. They even refused to
allow Polish planes carrying supplies from airfields in
England to embattled Warsaw to land for refueling on
the Russian-held airfields which were only a few minutes'
flying time from the flaming city. Some Polish planes
flew in anyway to parachute supplies to the Warsaw in-

surgents. They ran the gauntlet of German fighters for a thousand miles, then dipped low to drop the supplies into the liberated sections of the city. As they descended, the planes were shot down by German anti-aircraft guns. If they tried to drop the parachutes from a safe height, the summer breeze carried the supplies over to German lines. The battle for Warsaw was turning into a massacre of the rebels.

A month later Warsaw was nothing but smoldering ruins. The insurrection ended in the complete defeat of the Polish rebels. The Germans rounded up the survivors and took them to prisoner-of-war camps, leaving the civilian population to its fate in the ancient city. Less than five out of every hundred buildings still stood. There was neither food nor water, and the streets and ruins of Warsaw were littered with corpses. Only then did the Russians move forward. They now were able to "liberate" Poland's capital from the weakened German forces with no difficulty.

Soon the "Lublin Committee" was set up as Poland's provisional government. The lawful government, and the Polish armies which were fighting in the west, remained in exile. The surviving members of Polish resistance who had been evading the Germans for many years were now hunted down by the Russians. Poland was brought under a new yoke, and the development of the communist system began.

9

Postwar Poland

POLAND EMERGED reeling from World War II. Seldom in its thousand-year history had the outcome of a war been as disastrous, and never had the devastation and loss of life been as great. Over ten per cent of Poland's population had died in the war, and hundreds of thousands more were dislocated from their homes. Many thousands who had been deported to Germany remained abroad as refugees, joining former prisoners of war released at the end of the war and the members of Polish armies which had fought—and remained—in the west. There was a bitter irony in the fact that Poland, the country which was the first to become engaged in the war against the Nazis and which had suffered the longest and harshest occupation, failed to regain its freedom after the enemy's surrender. The peace that war's end had brought to Poland was a tormented peace. Soviet armies and diplomacy brought the communists to power in Poland shortly after World War II. For many years these armies remained stationed in Poland, as well as in East Germany to the west and, later on, in Czechoslovakia to the south of Poland. After 1948, all Poland's borders were shared with countries of the Soviet bloc. Nevertheless, the Polish Communists could not—for a while—win complete control over the unwilling nation. There were several powerful forces within Poland which had to be taken into account. One of them was the Roman Catholic Church. Among the others were two major political parties—the Polish Peasant Party and the Polish Socialist Party. These two parties far outnumbered the Communist Party, but they lacked the power that the communists drew from Russia's support.

This situation forced the communists to share the government, at least nominally, with the other major political forces for over two years. Then, in 1947, the Socialist Party split and one of its wings joined with the communists, who thus gained enough strength to cast off the remaining socialists and the Peasant Party. The only organized force still opposing the Communists was the Roman Catholic Church.

Under the Yalta Agreement, Poland lost some territories but gained others. A belt about 50 to 150 miles wide along Poland's eastern border was transferred to Russia. On the other hand, some of the ancient Polish territories held by Germany were now restored to Poland. This included parts of East Prussia and Pomerania in the north. At last, Poland once again had more than a mere foothold on the Baltic coast at Gdynia. Now Poland's coast extended from the Gulf of Danzig in the east for over 250 miles to the west, and in addition to Gdynia it included the major ports of Gdansk, the former Danzig, and Szczecin, the former Stettin in the west, as well as a number of smaller ports and seaside resorts. Along her western borders, Poland reacquired most of Silesia, an area rich in ores, especially coal, that also included such industrial centers as Wroclaw, the former Breslau. Poland's western border with Germany followed the line of the rivers Oder and Neisse.

Wroclaw, now a major industrial city in Poland, was once known as Breslau.

The German-speaking people fled from the regions acquired by Poland at the end of the war, with few exceptions, leaving behind their empty farms and ghost-like towns, many of which were in ruins. Resettled into this empty land were Poles from the eastern territories that had been lost to Russia. They began building their lives anew, reclaiming the fields, rebuilding the farms and towns, reopening the mines, and reactivating industries. This was their new homeland. They pushed their roots deep into its soil and, paying little attention to domestic politics, developed the land with the enthusiasm of pioneers. Their pioneering spirit attracted a great many younger people from all over Poland, and they, too, came to settle here. For a long time Poland's western territories had the nation's youngest population, and the freest spirit as well. Here, they were building their lives with much hope for the future, they worked hard, and if their daily lives were without many amenities, they did not mind it. They knew that Germany would continue to claim this land, but they also knew that they would not yield it easily to anyone, whether another country or the Polish Communists. In the 1950's as well as in the 1960's and even the 1970's, it was in this region that the government encountered dangerous opposition to some of its policies, opposition which would force changes affecting the whole of Poland.

As expected, Germany refused for many years to accept the loss of Silesia to Poland and to recognize the Oder-Neisse boundary. East Germany, a Soviet satellite, recognized the Oder-Neisse boundary under pressure from Russia, but West Germany did not until the early 1970's. Many Poles believed that their new acquisitions could remain secure only with Russia's continued support, and in return many were willing to go along with the Russians' Communist allies in Poland. For many, security of Poland's new borders justified its close and dependent, even if uncomfortable and unequal, relationship with the USSR. It was probably this more than any other consideration that made some members of the Polish Socialist and Peasant parties side with the Communists in the early postwar years.

There remained yet another set of problems—the reconstruction of a devastated land. In Poland, the war front had crossed the country twice—first during the Nazi advance eastward in 1939–1941, and then again during the Soviet advance westward in 1944–1945. Never before had a nation been exposed to the shock of devastating modern warfare between two immensely powerful adversaries to the degree that Poland was—and, worst of all, neither the Germans nor the Russians had any friendly feeling for the Poles in whose land and cities they fought.

Throughout Poland the towns and cities, ports, roads, railroads and bridges, tunnels, water supply systems, underground sewage pipes, industrial plants and electric power stations, mine shafts, buildings, and even pavement in the streets were in ruins. Industrial equipment, farm machines, railroad rolling stock, trucks, and most automobiles had been either requisitioned and removed from

Poland, or wrecked in fighting. Museums, as well as homes, had been looted by the armies. Farm produce was taken away or destroyed. And there were thousands upon thousands of homeless families as the war drew to its end. Warsaw, Poland's capital and the symbol of its independence, had no more than 10 percent of its buildings still standing, and even these had been heavily damaged. The city had suffered much for six years: first the Nazi assault in 1939, with aerial and artillery bombardment, then the occupation. The Jewish ghetto, which the Nazis had walled in before moving against its starving inhabitants, had been demolished during desperate attempts to fight back and resist deportation to the death camps. Of the thousands of families that had been driven into the ghetto, less than a dozen people survived. The long weeks and months of the Warsaw Insurrection followed in August and September 1944: days and nights of close-range Nazi bombardment, and the slow Nazi advance against the insurgents with methodical dynamiting of buildings, block by block and street by street, until nothing but smoldering ruins and corpses was left.

Against this background of devastation, politics and ideologies mattered little; it was amazing that the Poles found enough spirit left in themselves to struggle for their political future even then.

Help arrived quickly. The United Nations Relief and Rehabilitation Administration, known as the UNRRA, brought food supplies, mostly from the United States, and farm equipment, tools, trucks, and railroad rolling stock followed. Poland also collected war reparations. In return for some of the Polish industrial plants which had been dismantled and removed to Germany, Poland collected German plants, which were transferred to Polish factories. All this helped, but the main effort naturally had to come from the exhausted Polish nation itself. Many miracles were performed in this effort to rebuild Poland, but perhaps the greatest miracle of all was accomplished in the reconstruction of Warsaw.

Since war had left Warsaw nothing but an expanse of rubble, many people held that the site of the ancient capital should be abandoned, and a new city built elsewhere. But Warsaw for the Poles is more than a city. It is a symbol of past glory and greatness as the city of kings and poets, of composers and authors, a symbol of determination to survive no matter what odds. Even now, at the end of the war, Warsaw was like Poland itself—wholly in ruins but refusing to die. Warsaw, most people held, must be rebuilt as a symbol of Poland reborn. And not only rebuilt, but it must be made the city it once was, and even better and lovelier than before. Passionate feeling prevailed over cold reason and the cost of rebuilding.

Old city maps and plans of historic districts in the Old Town were assembled painstakingly. Paintings and architectural sketches of ornamental exteriors of buildings and monuments, as well as panoramic views of the city, were found, or borrowed from museums and archives abroad. Then the architects and city planners drew new plans in which the old districts with their original streets would

Rubble piled high in the streets of Warsaw after the war.

be restored, while the Old Town would be surrounded by a well-planned modern city. Thus the symbol of the past would be cradled within the promise of the future.

The reconstruction of the Old Town included the salvaging of whatever original parts could be found. Decorative stone sculpture and ornamentation, parts of destroyed marble staircases or balconies, and even original bricks and roof tiles whenever they could be found in the rubble, were salvaged and reused. Regardless of their profession or trade, people—especially the young—threw themselves into the work. Little by little the winding cobbled streets with their picturesque buildings rose again from the rubble. On the outside, they look exactly as they did long ago. Inside, however, they are better than originally, since they now include fireproofing and other modern conveniences. The effort was immense and the cost incalculable, but the people of Poland gave willingly even in time of great adversity. Warsaw rose from the dust ready for the future without forgetting its past, from which the city and the nation draw their strength.

Warsaw restored—King Sigismund Column in Castle Square.

As the passing of time began healing the wounds of war and making the recollection of horrors somewhat remote, Poland's communist government started to develop its system. The nationalization and government operation of industry and business was only one of the means used toward developing the essential feature of a communist-ruled society, where all personal income would come from government-controlled sources. When a man's livelihood is thus controlled, his opposition to the program can be checked with ease.

The nationalization of industry, transportation, public utilities, banking and business was as swift as it was simple. It was done by decrees and laws which were passed by the communist-dominated parliament. Gradually people in the trades, professions, and arts were brought under government control as well. Tradesmen were forced into cooperatives that took over their shops, which then employed their former owners. Professional people and those in the arts were brought into government-controlled associations which not only licensed their members but also provided them with salaries.

Poland's once-famous arts became almost dormant as people were forced to follow the Soviet style of "socialist realism." This meant that art in all its forms had to serve the single purpose of communist political propaganda. The loss of creative freedom was deeply resented in the land which, for centuries, had been the eastern outpost of western culture. Now Poland was forced to sever its cultural ties with the west and even with its own past.

Yet, as long as Poland's agriculture remained beyond the communist control, the new system could not be firmly established. Over one-half of Poland's population were farmers who owned their property. Their livelihood was wholly independent of government-controlled wages and salaries. In the late 1940's, in order to take firm hold on the farmers and in the hope of improving the nation's agricultural output, the government started the program of farm collectivization.

This meant that farmers had to yield the property they owned to the collective farms set up in the villages. Then the farmers were employed by the collective as hired hands to till the land which was no longer theirs. The government would thus acquire control over their livelihood, while the pooling of small farms into large collectivized ones would permit efficient use of farm machines, reduce manpower requirements, and release many people from rural areas to work in industry. But the farmers were reluctant to give up their property and their economic independence.

In order to force the farmers to join the collectives, price controls kept farm produce at prices so low as to make private farming unprofitable. Taxes were raised and laws were passed requiring farmers to deliver to the government designated amounts of produce after each harvest. Farm tools, fertilizer, and consumer goods were rationed so that many necessities could be made unavailable to those farmers who refused to join collective farms. By the early 1950's most of Polish farm land was collectiv-

ized, but instead of improved output there was a cata-
strophic decline in food supply.

Poland, a country which once had had surplus food to
export, now did not have enough to feed its own growing
population. Those few farmers who still owned their property produced only that food which they needed for their
families plus, of course, the amounts they had to deliver
to the government. The output of the collective farms
was low because the farmers who had been forced into
them had no heart in their work.

Poland's industrial output in the new system was also
low and quality of goods poor. Wages were kept at a low
level. In order to get even this wage in full, men had to
work six days a week and, furthermore, had to produce
a designated amount of goods in that time. Government
economic plans fixed these amounts, called "production
norms," for every plant and every job in the land. If one
failed to meet the norm, his wage was cut proportionately,
and if this failure was repeated he could be shipped off to
a forced-labor camp and imprisoned without trial for an
indefinite term.

Dissatisfaction was widespread in Poland, until conditions changed in the Soviet Union, causing changes in
other communist lands. Russian dictator Joseph Stalin
died in the spring of 1953. His successors realized that if
any progress was to be achieved by the communist-con-
trolled countries, the restrictive "Stalinist" system in industry and agriculture had to be replaced by one which
gave people a greater incentive to work. This required re-

laxation of controls, rescinding oppressive laws and opening up greater opportunities for individuals.

Collectivization was discontinued and some property restrictions lifted. This made farming profitable again. People withdrew in droves from collective farms, returned to work and made Poland's food supplies so great that once again there were food surpluses to export.

In industry, however, production norms were relaxed, but wage controls remained unchanged while prices continued to rise. Thus, more than ten years after the communists had come to power, the Polish industrial workers were worse off than they had been before the war. In theory, they were now supposed to be a privileged class benefiting from revolutionary changes, but in fact their earnings—even when free medical treatment and hospitalization, paid vacations, and controlled rents were accounted for—amounted to about three-fourths of what they had been earning for similar work before the war. In the summer of 1956 the people in the city of Poznan, an industrial center in western Poland, rebelled against the government policies. Supported by people elsewhere, they called a strike. Several people, mostly young, were killed as troops rushed in. An angry populace attacked tanks with rocks and homemade weapons. The irate workers were pacified only when their demands for improvements were at least partially granted. Their real wages were raised—although this gain was to vanish before long, as inflationary trends continued in Poland— and they were permitted to organize "workers' councils."

It was hoped that these councils would become institutions of self-management with authority to decide a plant's policy and hire or dismiss its director, as well as to supervise the plant's hiring policies or resolve individual employee's grievances, and, most important, decide whether profits should be reinvested or used for housing, or even distributed among the employees as bonuses. This system of self-management held much promise. It could make industrial production responsive to the needs of the consumer, and by providing the incentive of bonuses, improve the quality of manufacturing. All this, however, rested upon the resolving of one essential question: Would the "workers' councils" really be freely elected, and would they really have the powers promised to them? For some fifteen years after 1956, the answer to this question remained unclear at best. The problem eventually led to the fall of Gomulka's government.

Nevertheless, after October 1956 the Polish people were full of hope for a better future and began pressing for greater liberty. Young Polish writers asked a question which would reverberate throughout the Communist lands from then on: Is it possible to have a Communist system without poverty, without social injustice, and without tyranny? Supported by a majority of the people, the writers demanded not only improvements in the economic system but also the abolition of the secret police, the immediate removal of Russian troops from Poland, and the dismissal of Soviet officers from the leading positions in the Polish armed forces. Responding to these demands,

Gomulka relieved Soviet Marshal Konstantin Rokossovsky of his posts. The marshal had been made Poland's minister of defense and commander-in-chief of the Polish armed forces some ten years earlier. Russian forces remained stationed in Poland, although their numbers were reduced.

The secret police organization was so powerful that it was no longer clear whether it was still an agency of the government, or had become an agency which controlled the government, the Communist Party, and the nation itself. What had become clear was that the main responsibility of the secret police was not just to stop all political dissent, but to prevent it. Eventually the police began deciding who might in the future become a dissenter, and checking him before he had reached that point with "preventive detention." The likelihood of such future dissent was estimated by the way a person criticized the government or life in Poland, by the kind of company he kept—it became dangerous indeed to have "wrong" friends—by his interest in events abroad or in modern art or music, even by the way he dressed or activities in which he did not participate. Almost anything could arouse the secret police's suspicion, and no one was safe from possible imprisonment; an innocent remark or a joke could be as dangerous as disagreement with policy by a Communist Party member in the councils. Wladyslaw Gomulka had been a prisoner of the Polish secret police. He was held without trial and tortured until shortly before he came to power.

What the people of Poland demanded in 1956 was an

end to this reign of terror that spared no one and an immediate return to a system under which, in accordance with Polish law, no one could be sentenced without trial and without opportunity to defend himself against the charges. Even the Polish Communist Party became divided on this issue. One wing stood for continued suppression of dissent and for the harsh "Stalinist" policies, while another wing was willing to grant some popular demands. This wing, led by Gomulka, prevailed and came to power in a bloodless revolution in October 1956. Secret police power was severely curtailed, but the organization itself was not disbanded, and its head, Mieczyslaw Moczar, would remain an important man in Poland for another fifteen years. Still, this was a long step toward improvement since "administrative sentencing" was virtually discontinued.

Poland's postwar period of reconstruction and search for a system that would be at least partly acceptable to majority of people ended with these changes. With the coming of Gomulka's government, people's hopes rose high. In economic affairs, there was hope for relative prosperity through impending management reforms. In political affairs, moderates had replaced the radicals, Russians were no longer in control of the armed forces, and relations between the government and the Roman Catholic Church improved after Gomulka released from detention Cardinal Wyszynski, the head of the Polish Church. Censorship and other restrictions upon the press were relaxed, and this was soon followed by the end of restrictions in publishing, in the arts, and in theater.

Life was still hard in Poland. More than ten years after the end of the war, Polish industrial workers could buy for their earnings only about three-fourths of what they could buy before the war; that is, their "real wages" were only about three-fourths of what they had been. This situation was true in all walks of life, but it did not matter much to the Poles. They had been successful in forcing changes in the system despite its power, despite Russia, and despite Poland's unfavorable geographical position in the postwar world.

10

Contemporary Poland

LIKE REBORN WARSAW, Poland today is a blend of modern and traditional. Its population is well above thirty-two million and it has a very high percentage of young people, most of whom have no personal recollection of the war and postwar years. It is a nation with a youthful outlook, its schools and streets full of young people whose tastes in dress follow closely and swiftly all changes in styles in the West. It is a nation in which there is a steady flow of people coming to live in the cities as they abandon their farms in the villages. Poland once again produces more food than it needs but it is no longer a predominantly agricultural country. Despite the many reversals and difficulties, the Poles have made their country an industrial one. Poland's industrial plants, supplied mainly by local coal, ores, and raw materials, now manufacture countless products for export as well as domestic needs. Products include electrical equipment, huge generators, and modern rolling stock for electrified railroads; steel for construction, bridges, and industry; textiles and fashionable clothing; complex produce of chemical industry; automobiles and trucks; aircraft and airplane engines. And since the major ports of Gdansk and Szczecin with their shipyards have been added to those in Gdynia, its shipbuilding and shipping industries now carry the Polish flag across all the oceans.

Economic development and industrial growth require trained people, of course. Poland's industrial skills were inherited from its labor force trained before the war, and complemented by new workers trained within a broad educational system. Grade school education for all is required by law. There are only public schools; private and parochial schools have been disbanded. After grade school, those young people who do not return to the farm are given opportunities to take vocational training for jobs in industry, or for high school preparatory to higher education in universities. Poland's oldest, largest, and most renowned universities are in Warsaw and Cracow, but there are others in Lodz, Poznan, Torun, Wroclaw in the west, and Lublin in the east.

Elementary schools are tuition-free and about four of every five university students receive government scholarships which, though modest, suffice to cover the student's living expenses. While in theory schooling was open to all qualified young people, in fact for many years considerations other than grades and ability determined admission to higher education. Until 1956, and to lesser degree thereafter, students with "undesirable social origin"—that is, the sons and daughters of former government officials, army officers, businessmen, or anyone who was suspect by the secret police—were denied admission to the universities. Also, the student did not have free choice of the field of study he would pursue. The government decided each year which occupations or professions could be expected to need more trained people in the future, and the students were enrolled accordingly. Thus, a student who qualified for admission to a medical school often found himself instead in the school of engineering or accounting. Once enrolled, he was not free to change schools, and upon graduation he was assigned employment anywhere in Poland. He had to stay in the assigned employment generally for as many years as he had been studying in the university, and if he was on scholarship, even longer.

Restrictions in industry were similar. Once employed, a worker was not permitted to resign, nor could anyone employ him unless he produced written permission from his previous employer to leave his job. Such permission was very difficult to obtain, especially in the case of the younger and more promising workers. These restrictions caused much restlessness among the young people, both in industry and among the recent university graduates. Restrictions were never abandoned, but they were relaxed little by little during the 1960's. Even in the 1970's, however, no employee could leave the premises of a plant during his shift without special written permission.

The enthusiasm with which the Poles greeted the end of the postwar years in 1956 was dampened when developments did not rise to expectations. But then these expectations largely failed to take into account the realities of Poland's international commitments, which, now as always, produce a decisive effect on life in Poland.

In the fall of 1947, the Soviet Union organized a meeting of several Communist parties. It was held in Poland, and was attended by representatives of nearly all East European Communist parties, as well as those of France and Italy. At this meeting a new international organization, the Communist Information Bureau, or Cominform, was formed. Ostensibly, this organization was supposed only to exchange information and coordinate activities of the many Communist parties. In fact, however, it was controlled by the Russians and used by them for continuous supervision of other Communists. Less than a year later the Cominform began to fall apart, but only one member country, Yugoslavia, succeeded in breaking away. Although Poland disliked this organization quite as much, the fact that Poland was surrounded by the Soviet-controlled countries precluded its breaking away.

While Western Europe, in the early postwar years, moved toward economic integration through the Common Market, Russia tried to develop a similar organization in Eastern Europe. This was the Council for Mutual Economic Assistance, or Comecon. Poland was among the first countries to join. It soon became clear that Comecon was very different from the Common Market, and that its member countries were expected to direct their own development mainly to help the economy of the Soviet Union. In general, both the Cominform and the Comecon were organizations which viewed the entire Soviet bloc as a single political and economic entity in which each member was expected to work to advance the development of the strongest member of this entity, that is, the Soviet Union.

Then, in 1955, these political and economic organizations were complemented by a military one—the Warsaw Treaty Organization. This treaty provided for mutual defense and close coordination of the armed forces of its members, joint military planning, and frequent military exercises to which most or all of the members would bring units of their armed forces.

What many people had suspected about the purpose of this organization was confirmed many years later. In 1968, the Communists in Czechoslovakia attempted to reform the Communist system so as to remove injustice and tyranny from it and, as they said, to give it "a humane face." People in Czechoslovakia supported this change with great enthusiasm, but in August 1968 the Soviet Union called for "military exercises" of the Warsaw Treaty Organization to be held in Poland. Then, suddenly, the armed forces which had been assembled for exercises—the Russian units were by far the strongest and most numerous—were ordered to invade Czechoslovakia, whose government was changed by force as strict party adherents were brought in to replace the moderates. The Soviet Union's ominous explanation for this was not lost on Poland. East European countries were told that within the Warsaw Treaty Organization the national sovereignty of its members is limited. They may be independent and sovereign, but not to the point of instituting reforms regarded as dangerous by other members. This "limited sovereignty" gives other members the right to invade a country if it insists on reforms.

After this experience, the few remaining liberal reforms from 1956 were reduced to insignificance, and a great many people in Poland became disillusioned with Gomulka. In their eyes, he was so afraid of Russia that he could no longer do what was necessary for Poland, and had even allowed Poland to be a part of the invasion of a friendly neighbor, Czechoslovakia. So again the clouds of troubled times covered Polish sky—prices kept rising but wages remained controlled and frozen, censorship reappeared, and General Mieczyslaw Moczar's secret police made its presence felt more and more. Once again an air of listlessness fell over the people. There were shortages of food and fuel supplies as 1970 drew to its end, and people awaited with apprehension the coming of another harsh winter. For some time, workers in many plants and mines had tried to seek solutions to their grievances by going on strike, and each time they were suppressed by force—with increasing violence. Then, some ten days before Christmas 1970, there came a government announcement of a large price increase for food and basic commodities. Infuriated, the shipyard workers in Gdansk went on strike. The strike spread to the neighboring shipyards in Gdynia, and then to plants throughout the country. The government replied by sending in police and troops with tanks and machine guns, which only added fuel to the fury of thousands of shipyard workers. Before long, masses of people were streaming through the streets of Baltic ports, trying to break into prisons to free those who had been arrested, setting fire to local Communist Party headquarters buildings, and, in turn, being exposed to machine-gun fire both from the ground and from government helicopters hovering just above the roofs. Strikes spread from Gdansk and Gdynia to Szczecin, and then inland to the industrial centers of Katowice and Poznan, and even to the large automobile manufacturing plants in the suburbs of Warsaw.

It appeared that Poland was on the eve of a revolution—a revolution that would overthrow Gomulka, but would, with equal certainty, lead to the entry of Soviet troops. But then, on December 20, Gomulka's resignation was announced. The aging, ill man who once was seen as harbinger of liberty in Poland resigned amid gunfire and burning buildings in a land where once again men had to fight for their rights against insuperable odds.

Wladyslaw Gomulka was replaced by Edward Gierek, an engineer who had lived for many years in Western Europe. This change produced neither rising expectations nor outbursts of creativity as the change in 1956 had done, but it avoided armed intervention from abroad and held some promise for economic improvements. And, in fact, before too long Gierek brought forth improvements. The announced rise in prices was abolished, the striking workers were not persecuted, and a new Five-Year Plan directing Poland's industrial production away from heavy industry and toward the manufacturing of consumer goods was announced.

In the meanwhile, Poland finally concluded a treaty

with West Germany, in which West Germany recognized as final the Polish border on the Oder and Neisse rivers. This removed a threat which had hung over Poland for over twenty-five years, and soon afterward, in a conciliatory move, Gierek granted the Polish Church the full title to church property—thousands of parish buildings, chapels, churches, and other property—in the western territories Poland had acquired after World War II. This was followed by Gierek's removal of General Moczar and most of his key officers from the secret police, some of whom were even arrested on charges of corruption. Poland found itself on the threshold of yet another age in her long history.

As with all countries in the world, Poland's future lies with its young people. They were born since the end of World War II, yet they too have known hardships—hardships of poverty, of injustice and restrictions, and danger. Perhaps because of this, Poland's young people seem to be hard realists when it comes to the issues of survival, as well as rather poetic and always witty dreamers when it comes to their daily lives. They are all immensely proud of being Polish, but their patriotism does keep them from criticizing what they find objectionable in their country. They are on the whole surprisingly well-informed about the outside world, and at the time when unrest and rioting was sweeping the schools and universities in the West, in the late 1960's and early 1970's, Polish students said on many occasions, always with a wry smile, that the liberties which others take for granted are those for which they, the Poles, are struggling.

INDEX

About the Authors

Born in Massachusetts, Eric P. Kelly was graduated from Dartmouth College and spent some years as a newspaper reporter before returning to Dartmouth to teach. His first association with the Polish people was when, during World War I, he was sent to Brittany to serve as physical and recreational director for American-Polish Servicemen there. Then, when the Bolshevik war began, Mr. Kelly accompanied the American Poles who hurried to Poland to help their country win their struggle against the Russians. Because of his continued interest in Poland after his return to the United States, the author was sent by the Kosciuszko Foundation as a student and lecturer on American literature to the University of Krakow. And, finally, at the end of World War II, he was sent by the United States government to establish a camp for refugees from war-torn Poland in Mexico.

Dragos D. Kostich is professor of interdisciplinary studies and director of area study programs at the Brooklyn Center of Long Island University. Born and raised in Belgrade, Yugoslavia, he served in the Yugoslav Air Force and in the Resistance during World War II; he was imprisoned in a concentration camp from which he escaped and rejoined the underground. He holds degrees from the University of Paris, and is an expert on the history and government of Eastern Europe and Russia. He has taught at the New School for Social Research in New York City, where he was also associate dean, and is the author of *The Land and People of the Balkans,* as well as many articles and book reviews.